College Student
Psychological Adjustment

College Student Psychological Adjustment

Exploring Relational Dynamics that Predict Success

Jonathan F. Mattanah

MP MOMENTUM PRESS
HEALTH

MOMENTUM PRESS, LLC, NEW YORK

College Student Psychological Adjustment: Exploring Relational Dynamics that Predict Success

Copyright © Momentum Press, LLC, 2016.

First published in 2016 by
Momentum Press, LLC
222 East 46th Street, New York, NY 10017
www.momentumpress.net

ISBN-13: 978-1-60650-007-1 (paperback)
ISBN-13: 978-1-60650-010-1 (e-book)

Momentum Press Psychology Collection

Cover and interior design by Exeter Premedia Services Private Ltd., Chennai, India

First edition: 2016

10 9 8 7 6 5 4 3 2 1

Printed in the United States of America.

Abstract

Although students are attending college at higher rates in the United States than at any other time in history, not all are doing well once they get there. In fact, only about 60 percent of students, initially entering college, graduate within four to six years; many other students struggle with significant mental health difficulties while in college. What we know is that students' relationships with close others, including their parents, faculty mentors, friends, and romantic partners, are important determinants of how well they are able to navigate the pathway through college. The current book examines the dynamics of healthy relationship formation with each of these important individuals in a student's life and the impact of those relationship dynamics on students' academic, social, and emotional adjustment to college. Aimed at advanced undergraduates, graduate students, and scholars in the fields of psychology, human development, and higher education, the author reviews a wealth of contemporary and classic research studies that demonstrate clear and consistent links between relationship development and psychological growth and adjustment for college students. Ultimately, readers in the fields of mental health and higher education will gain a fresh perspective on the relationship development of college students and possible avenues for intervention to help students enhance their relationship skills in order to prevent the development of mental health difficulties in college.

Keywords

college student adjustment, emerging adulthood, family dynamics, interracial friendship formation, marital conflict, parent–student attachment relationships, relationship enhancement interventions, romantic relationship competence, roommate relationships, student–faculty relationships

Contents

Preface

More students are attending college in the United States today than at any other point in this country's history. And, as I document in my other book on this topic, campus communities are becoming increasingly diverse, including larger numbers of ethnic minority students, women, and students with physical and mental disabilities (Mattanah 2016). The diversity and greater inclusiveness of institutions of higher learning are cause for celebration, and the number of students matriculating into higher education attests to the importance of this developmental milestone for the lives of young people.

Unfortunately, not all students who enter college graduate. In fact, the statistics on four-to-six year graduation rates are sobering. Only about 60 percent of students who enter college will graduate within six years (NCES Condition of Education Report 2014). Moreover, while at university, many students struggle with significant symptoms of stress, anxiety, and depression, some so profound that they even consider taking their own lives (Mattanah 2016).

What makes college so stressful and why do 40 percent of students not make it through? Those are the questions that inspired the writing of this book. As a university professor and clinical psychologist, I have been studying college student adjustment for the past 15 years. The consistent pattern I have discovered in my research is that it is the *relationships* that students form while at college that most profoundly determine whether students succeed or fail and whether they remain or leave. My own research, and a wealth of other studies I review in this book, has found that students who form supportive, nurturing relationships with their professors, fellow students, romantic partners, and even administrative support staff at the university, feel socially and emotionally integrated into the campus community and thereby succeed academically as well. Students who fail to make those pivotal connections on campus end up feeling isolated and disengaged, and are at risk for developing psychological symptoms of distress and ultimately leaving the university.

The Scope of This Book

The current book traces the importance of students' relational functioning across five pivotally important relationships within college life. In Chapter 1, I discuss the ongoing importance of the parent–student relationship for the well-being of students while in college. Chapter 1 also examines the importance of faculty–student relationships in predicting students' social and academic success in college. Chapter 2 focuses on students' peer relationships, examining three key peer groups that all students encounter in college, namely, roommates, friends, and romantic partners. This chapter also explores how students are negotiating the changing landscape of romantic and sexual encounters in the 21st century. Finally, Chapter 3 examines intervention programs that have been developed on college campuses to teach students relationship skills. These interventions are quite novel and represent a type of preventative intervention strategy, targeting a wide cross-section of students who might never seek counseling services but who can benefit from being taught skills that may improve their functioning and prevent problems down the road.

This book, in conjunction with my other book on the topic, *College Student Psychological Adjustment: Theory, Method, and Statistical Trends*, provide the reader a thorough introduction to the study of college student adjustment, understanding trends in college attendance, theories of college student development, methods for studying adjustment, and, in this book, examining relational dynamics that predict academic, social, and emotional adjustment to college.

Acknowledgments

I wish to thank a number of people who helped in the completion of this project. First, I thank my two external reviewers and colleagues, Laura Holt and Christa Schmidt, who read the entire manuscript and provided detailed feedback. I would also like to thank professors Christine Allegretti and Melinda Harper for taking the time to discuss their efforts to implement the Transition to University (T2U) intervention program at Queens University in Charlotte, NC.

I am grateful to Jennifer Daks, my former student, for her excellent feedback on the manuscript. In addition, I have worked with many other students over the years who served as inspiration for many of the ideas I discuss in this book. I am grateful to them all.

I also extend my gratitude to the helpful editorial staff at Momentum Press who helped shuttle this project to its completion. In particular, I acknowledge Shoshanna Goldberg who first approached me with the idea of writing this book, and Peggy Williams, senior editor at Momentum Press, who has been a great help in conceptualizing this project and fashioning it in its final form.

Finally, I am deeply grateful to my family for their love and support throughout this project. I appreciate them putting up with my changing moods as I worked on these two books and tolerating my occasional lectures. My hope for my adolescent children is that as they approach college age they will have the wisdom to value their relationships highly and integrate themselves into their communities, so that they, too, can succeed in whatever they choose to do.

CHAPTER 1

The Impact of Parent– Student and Faculty– Student Relationships on College Adjustment

You can rarely open a newspaper today without reading about some new study examining the ways in which parents are upsetting their college students! Most of the press coverage is quite negative, depicting parents as hovering over their college students, interfering in ways they should not, like calling their student's professor to complain about a grade or telling their child whom to choose as friends and what they should and should not eat in the dining hall (Joyce 2014). These "helicopter parents" are contrasted with "free-range parents" who are so lackadaisical that they dare never tell their child anything they are doing wrong, preferring for their student to learn and adapt entirely on their own (Joyce 2015). Such news reports surely reflect the level of anxiety the public feels about the lives of college students, most particularly, parents who are seeking guidance about what their role should be once their 18-year-old child has left home to attend college.

The reality is that college students continue to value their relationship with their parents once in college. They turn to their parents for support, guidance, advice, and emotional re-fueling. Although some parental behaviors can be problematic for the development of college students, such as helicopter parenting, the problem is overstated, as most parent–student relationships are nurturing and some level of parental involvement is quite welcomed by young college students. In this chapter, I examine the impact of the parent–student relationship on student functioning and development. In the last section of the chapter, I will also discuss the importance of the faculty–student relationship for students' adjustment to college.

The Parent–Student Attachment Relationship

The first way in which the parent–student relationship has been studied with college students has been to focus on their attachment relationship. This work is based on the theorizing of John Bowlby, a British psychoanalyst who suggested that infants and young children form attachment relationships with their caregivers in order to aid in their survival (Bowlby 1969/1982). Although the attachment relationship is formed in infancy it is important throughout the lifespan, in part because the developing child forms a mental representation of their relationship with their caregiver, called an internal working model of their attachment relationship. For children with secure relationships with their parents, their model of relationships is that they are enriching, enjoyable, and worthwhile. Individuals with a history of less comforting parent–child interactions may develop insecure internal working models, in which they view themselves as worthless, see others as unavailable or untrustworthy, and view relationships as fraught with danger or not worthwhile. Bowlby's theory of attachment was tested on young infants using the Strange Situation Paradigm designed by Mary Ainsworth. In the Strange Situation, the young infant's attachment system is activated by being put into an unusual environment, the introduction of a stranger, and eventually by being left entirely alone in this strange environment. As predicted, infants played while the mother was present, showed extreme distress when the mother was absent, and then were able to return to playing when the mother returned (Ainsworth et al. 1978, reprinted 2015).

The Transition to College as a Second Strange Situation

Kenny (1987) likened the transition to college to a second "strange situation" wherein the adolescent is leaving home for a strange environment and experiencing a significant separation from his or her parents, presumably much longer than any one experienced up to that point in the adolescent's life. Although college-bound adolescents seek to loosen ties with family, as they explore their identity in college, Kenny maintained that students also wish to retain their connection with their parents and will often turn to their parents for emotional re-fueling, much like the young child who seeks to master their environment while checking-in periodically with parents for support and comfort.

To examine the parent–student attachment relationship, Kenny created the Parental Attachment Questionnaire (PAQ). This measure focuses on three major aspects of the parent–student attachment relationship: (1) affective quality of the relationship, (2) parental fostering of child autonomy, and (3) providing emotional support. Hence, the PAQ reflects a balance of providing support and encouraging autonomy and independence. The PAQ is internally consistent and stable over a two-week period (Kenny 1987, 1990; Kenny and Donaldson 1991).

In a sample of 173 first-year college students, Kenny found that students rated their relationship with their parents as positive, answering questions on the PAQ with an average score of a four on a five-point scale (a four meant they agreed with the items of the PAQ "quite a bit"). Kenny found that men reported turning to their parents (the PAQ does not ask about mothers and fathers separately, as do other measures of attachment discussed later) for emotional support to a somewhat lesser extent than women (Kenny 1987).

Kenny found that students who reported a more secure attachment relationship with their parents also reported greater social competence with their peers, meaning that they were more willing to be assertive of their needs and felt more competent dating romantic partners. Additionally, students with more secure relationships with parents reported less distress during the transition to college (Kenny 1987; Kenny and Donaldson 1991). Kenny followed up her initial sample when they were seniors and found that students continued to report highly positive relationships with their parents. She found that college seniors with more secure attachment relationships reported a greater willingness and ability to engage in career planning as compared with less securely attached students (Kenny 1990). These results suggest that secure parent–student attachment relationships continue to matter throughout college but in developmentally salient ways, predicting social competence and less distress during the initial transition and a greater willingness to focus on career planning as students transition out of college.

Beyond Kenny: 30 Years of Research on the Parent–Student Attachment Relationship

Maureen Kenny's innovative application of attachment theory to college student relationships with their parents ignited an explosion of research over the past 30 years. When we conducted a meta-analysis of these studies in 2011, we were able to identify over 155 individual research studies that had been conducted examining the effects of attachment on some aspect of adjustment in college. This line of research has been aided by the development of a number of self-report measures of the parent–student attachment relationship beyond Kenny's PAQ. Probably the most widely used measure beside the PAQ is the Inventory of Parent and Peer Attachment (IPPA; Armsden and Greenberg 1987). Unlike the PAQ, the IPPA includes separate scales for attachment to mother and father, allowing researchers to do a more fine-grained analysis of links between specific parental attachment relationships and adjustment in men versus women. I turn now to a closer examination of the research on parent–student attachment relationships conducted in the past 30 years.

One major focus of this research has been to expand the range of outcomes linked with secure parental attachment relationships. Kenny and Rice (1995) argued that the positive internal working model of self that is the legacy of secure parent–child attachment may allow students to cope with disappointments that occur during the college experience, such as facing social rejection by peers or receiving a failing grade on an exam. Likewise, the positive model of others should allow students to feel more comfortable seeking help from faculty, staff, and other higher education personnel. These speculations have received empirical support in studies of parent–student attachment relationships and academic adjustment.

First, a number of studies have found that secure parent–student attachment relationships are associated with students feeling more confident about their academic work (Bell et al. 1996; Fass and Tubman 2002; Holt 2014). Second, studies have found that students more securely attached to their parents report using more action-oriented coping strategies, such as planning and problem-solving, rather than passive or distancing coping strategies, which seek to avoid problems by not thinking about them too much (Brack, Gay, and Matheny 1993; Greenberger and McLaughlin 1998). Clearly, students who use more active coping mechanisms are more likely to successfully solve academic challenges and ultimately to demonstrate better adjustment to the demands of the college environment. Finally, studies have found that a secure attachment relationship to parents is associated with greater willingness to seek help from peers, teachers, and even academic counselors (Holt 2014; Larose and Bernier 2001; Larose, Boivin, and Doyle 2001). In an innovative study, Larose, Boivin, and Doyle (2001) examined a group of academically at-risk students in Canada (these students had very low high school grade point averages (GPAs)) who were involved in an academic counseling program during their first semester of college. The students attended an average of 10 sessions with an academic counselor, who was usually a faculty member at the university, in which they discussed ways of feeling integrated into the campus community and specific strategies to solve academic, social, and emotional difficulties. Interestingly, students who reported more secure attachment to their mothers and fathers were more likely to seek support from their academic counselor after the program was over and they were more likely to view the counselor as sensitive and supportive of their needs. This study shows the importance of secure parental attachment relationships for facilitating better faculty relationships in college and thereby predicting academic success.

Beyond academic adjustment, secure parental attachment has been associated with important developmental concerns for college students. In one series of studies, Blazina and colleagues examined links between secure parent–student attachment relationships and the development of gender identity for men in particular (Blazina and Watkins 1996, 2000). Blazina argued that because of the unique situation in which men are raised by women (mothers) and then, as they mature, are urged to dis-identify and devalue the feminine, they often develop conflicted feelings about their gender role in society. Gender role conflict leads men to restrict their emotional expressions, devalue women, and, in turn, have difficulty interacting with women on college campuses. In a sample of male undergraduates, Blazina and Watkins (2000) found that men who reported more secure attachment relationships with their fathers also reported less "restricted emotionality," fewer negative feelings toward women, and also less endorsement of stereotypical masculine attitudes toward success, power, and competition. In turn, these men also reported fewer difficulties interacting with women. In an interesting follow-up study, researchers were able to show that men's level of gender role conflict was correlated with how conflicted they perceived their fathers to be with regard to their gender role as well. Men who perceived their fathers as having more gender role conflict also felt less securely attached and more psychologically separated from their fathers, which, in turn, negatively impacted their social adjustment in college (DeFranc and Mahalik 2002).

This research raises broader questions concerning the differential impact of secure attachment to mothers and fathers on men versus women's psychological development in college. Overall, women report feeling more securely attached to their parents than men do and they will check-in with their parents more often, just to give and receive emotional support (Kenny and Rice 1995; Sorokou and Weissbrod 2005). Although attachment to parents is important for psychological adjustment for both women and men, the patterns of results are different between the sexes. Women appear to seek emotional support from their mothers and fathers equally often and benefit from both supportive relationships with regard to a number of adjustment outcomes. Women with secure attachment to their mothers and fathers report greater social, emotional, and academic adjustment to college and form more secure relationships with their romantic partners (Carranza, Kilmann, and Vendemia 2009; Rice and Whaley 1993). Men, on the other hand, seem to rely on their parents' support particularly during stressful times, such as during final exam period (Rice and Whaley 1993).

Moreover, as already noted earlier, men appear to benefit especially from a secure attachment relationship with their fathers. In addition to the studies cited earlier, Blustein and colleagues found that men with a secure attachment to their fathers showed greater commitment to their career choices (Blustein et al. 1991). Additionally, for men from divorced households, more secure attachment and less hostility in their relationship with their fathers predicted men's ability to form a secure representation of attachment with regard to romantic partners (Carranza,

Kilmann, and Vendemia 2009). Perhaps these differential patterns of findings harken back to the theoretical suggestions of Blazina and colleagues. Because women experience less gender role conflict during development and are encouraged by society to form warm relationships with both their parents, they continue to rely on both parents during the college transition and reap benefits from those supportive relationships. By contrast, because men are encouraged to dis-identify with their early supportive relationship with their mothers, and often form conflicted relationships with their fathers, warm, nurturing father–son relationships are particularly predictive of healthy patterns of adjustment during the college years.

Finally, a number of studies have shown that parental attachment predicts greater willingness to seek help from faculty and peers, which, in turn, predicts better academic and social adjustment to the college campus (Holt 2014; Larose and Bernier 2001). These results suggest that academic and clinical counselors working with insecurely attached college students need to be aware that these students are likely to be hesitant to seek help from their teachers and friends but that encouraging them to do so will be quite helpful to their adjustment to college.

Parenting Behaviors and College Adjustment

A healthy attachment bond is one key component of a successful parent–student relationship during the college years. But, what about other parenting behaviors? How should parents engage with their college students to be most helpful and least harmful to their development during this time period? Recently, researchers have begun to examine parenting behaviors that predict good adjustment outcomes among emerging adult college students. I review some of this research in detail in the following.

Parenting Styles and College Adjustment

Researchers who are interested in examining ways in which parents promote optimal development in their offspring have focused on three major styles of parenting, identified as authoritarian, permissive, and authoritative (Baumrind 1971, 1989). Here is a brief description of each style:

1. **Authoritarian parenting**—Authoritarian parents highly value parental authority; they assert their authority over their child and teach their child to obey unquestioningly. These parents are highly controlling and do not encourage autonomy in their offspring. They also tend not to form a close, warm relationship with their child.

2. **Permissive parenting**—Permissive parents believe strongly in child self-determination and seek to guide their child without many rules or regulations. These parents encourage autonomy and do not control their child's behavior; they also tend to show a moderate degree of warmth and responsiveness to their child's needs.

3. **Authoritative parenting**—Authoritative parents also value authority but in a more child-centered manner. They will assert authority at times but will also consider the views of the child and are willing to engage their children in discussion and conversation with regard to decision-making. These parents control their child to some degree and display warmth/responsiveness to their child's needs. They also encourage age-appropriate autonomy in their children.

These styles of parenting have been researched heavily with child and adolescent samples, wherein children of authoritative parents have consistently fared better than children of authoritarian or permissive parents (Baumrind 1971, 1989; Lamborn et al. 1991; Steinberg, Elmen, and Mounts 1989). A small amount of research has examined the role of these parenting styles in predicting competence and adjustment among college students. Weiss and Schwarz (1996) measured parenting styles by both parent and child perception during the first year of college. Outcomes were assessed three years later, when the students were in their senior year of college. They found that males of authoritative households had the highest GPAs and were the least likely to use drugs while in college than any other parenting styles. Females from nondirective households, where parents were high on involvement and autonomy encouragement but low on strict control, had the highest GPAs but were only average on other adjustment outcomes. Across both men and women, children of authoritative, democratic, and nondirective parents (all of whom were high on support, involvement, and autonomy encouragement but varied in terms of how controlling they were) had the lowest levels of depression, neuroticism, and maladjustment when compared with children of authoritarian or disengaged households. Weiss and Schwarz's tentative conclusion from their results was that supportiveness and encouragement of autonomy may be the key components of success with college students; strict, directive control (as seen in authoritarian parenting) seems detrimental to development during this time period. We will see this theme come back again and again throughout this section.

Strage and Brandt (1999) found that all three dimensions of authoritative parenting were associated with greater academic motivation in a diverse sample of college juniors and seniors, including greater persistence at tasks, more academic confidence, and better rapport with teachers. Interestingly, however, only autonomy encouragement was associated with higher GPAs, and this was primarily true for students living on their own. This result harkens back to Weiss and Schwarz's conclusion that nondirective encouragement of autonomy is particularly helpful to college students (perhaps, especially college women) who are already showing signs of independence and who are achieving well.

In more recent years, researchers have argued that we need to identify the parenting styles that are most relevant to college student development, rather than assuming that concepts such as authoritative parenting, which were developed by studying children and adolescents, are necessarily relevant during this time period (Nelson et al. 2011). Nelson and Padilla-Walker have spear-headed a major, ongoing study of parenting during emerging adulthood titled Project READY (Researching Emerging Adult's Developmental Years), which currently includes over 700 students drawn from five college campuses across the United States. Data from this study was gathered from online surveys completed by students as well as their mothers and fathers, which is unusual for studies of parenting within college samples.

Nelson et al. (2011) used cluster analysis to identify particular patterns of parenting that were most relevant within their sample of college students. Like in Baumrind's work, they found an authoritative and a disengaged cluster, but they also found a controlling-indulgent cluster, in which parents were high on extreme forms of control, such as punishment and verbal hostility, but were also indulgent at times (endorsing items such as "I spoil my child at times" or "I give into my child when the child causes a commotion about something"). Finally, they found an inconsistent cluster among mothers, who were high on extreme control, indulgence, and responsiveness (these mothers were distinguished from the authoritative mothers who were not indulgent and who did not use extreme forms of control such as verbal hostility). Nelson et al. (2011) found that students of authoritative mothers and fathers showed the highest levels of self-worth and kindness and lowest levels of anxiety, depression, and impulsivity, although students of authoritative fathers did show somewhat higher drinking behavior. Interestingly, students with inconsistent mothers did not differ from students of authoritative mothers in their levels of self-worth, kindness, depression, anxiety, or impulsivity. Students from the controlling-indulgent households had the worst quality relationship with their parents and had the highest levels of depression, anxiety, and impulsivity. These results are consistent with those of Weiss and Schwarz (1996) in showing that it is the warmth and responsiveness dimension of parenting (on which both authoritative and inconsistent mothers were high) that is most predictive of positive outcomes among emerging adult college students, at least with regard to mothers. Similarly, punishment and punitive control, much like authoritarian parenting, is particularly unwelcomed by college students and detrimental to their functioning in college. It is interesting to note that controlling parents could also be indulgent at times, suggesting that these parents may have been struggling with how best to interact with their child, now that he or she has left for college. I will return to this point later.

A final study of parenting style with college students has examined what specific parenting behaviors might mediate the effectiveness of authoritative parenting on college student functioning (Wintre and Yaffe 2000). In a one-year longitudinal design from the fall to the spring semester of the first year of college, Wintre and Yaffe collected data on parenting style and specific parenting behaviors, such as parent–child discussions, reciprocity in the parent–child relationship, and social support by parents. These authors found that for women authoritative parenting predicted greater discussion between the parent and student and greater discussion directly predicted greater adjustment to college by the end of the school year. For men, authoritative parenting predicted greater reciprocity in the parent–student relationship, meaning that the student perceived his parent as respecting him and treating him more as an equal. Greater reciprocity, in turn, predicted better adjustment to college by the end of the year. Similar to other studies, they also found that authoritarian parenting by mothers directly predicted worse GPAs in women.

The conclusion across these studies of parenting style is that warmth, responsiveness, and encouragement of autonomy are particularly important dimensions within the parent–student relationship during college. Parents who are warm and responsive and foster discussion and mutual exchanges with their college students promote better academic functioning and greater individual adjustment. On the other hand, strict control and punishment are resented by college students and detrimental to their functioning at this point in their development. Although this result makes sense from a developmental perspective, it leaves open the possibility that parents may still wish to exert some control over their children's behavior. It is clear that once children move out of the house, parents have less day-to-day interaction with them and hence less control over their behavior. However, it is known that emerging adulthood is a time of experimentation and college students take risks, such as excessive drinking and drug use and engaging in risky sexual behaviors. Parents are increasingly aware of those risks and wish to assert some control over their emerging adult's choices (Urry, Nelson, and Padilla-Walker 2011). The next section explores parents' attempts to exert control over their emerging adults' behavior and the implications of those control efforts for developmental outcomes.

Parental Control and Developmental Outcomes in Emerging Adulthood

In the developmental literature, three distinct forms of parental control have been identified. The first one is behavioral control. In this form of control, the parent seeks to control the child's behavior directly, perhaps setting punishments for misbehavior or providing rewards for good behaviors. Behavioral control with adolescents is also seen through parental monitoring of their adolescent's activities, reflecting their knowledge of the child's whereabouts, the friends they are hanging out with, and whether they are involved with alcohol, drugs, or other risky behaviors.

The second form of control is psychological control, which refers to "control attempts that intrude into the psychological and emotional development of the child" (Barber 1996, 3296). Psychological control can take the form of guilt induction, threats to withdraw love if the child does not do what the parent wants, or controlling verbal exchanges. Finally, a third form of control that has been identified as unique to the emerging adulthood years is called helicopter parenting. I will define helicopter parenting in greater detail later, but in brief it refers to a type of overcontrolling and overly solicitous parenting behavior, in which the parent makes decisions for the child or intervenes on the child's behalf, in a way that appears developmentally inappropriate. Each of these forms of control has been studied with regard to its implications for college student adjustment and development.

Direct forms of behavioral control are not especially relevant once a student has left for college because the parent can no longer easily reward and punish daily behaviors. However, a particular form of behavior control, called parental knowledge, is still relevant during this time and turns out to be predictive of emerging adult's engagement in fewer risky behaviors (Padilla-Walker et al. 2008; Urry, Nelson, and Padilla-Walker 2011). Parental knowledge refers to the idea that the parent knows what his or her child is up to and in particular knows about the child's level of involvement in drugs, alcohol, and risky sexual activity. Padilla-Walker et al. (2008) found that father's knowledge (as reported by the child) predicted less drug use and fewer sexual partners. Similarly, mothers' knowledge (as reported by the parent) predicted less heavy drinking and fewer sexual partners. These results were true particularly in the context of a close parent–student relationship. Maternal knowledge in the context of a less close relationship was unrelated to risky outcomes.

In a second study with the same sample, Urry, Nelson, and Padilla-Walker (2011) examined what factors predicted parental knowledge of their children's activities. They found that the students' reports of a history of a close relationship with their parent and satisfaction in their current relationship with the parent predicted greater parental knowledge. These effects, in turn, were mediated by student self-disclosure to the parent. In other words, parents developed knowledge of their students' risky behaviors because the student was willing to tell their parents about them!

They told them because they felt good about their relationship with their parents, both in the past and present.

These results may seem obvious or intuitive but they are actually quite profound when considering the dilemma of parenting an emerging adult offspring. They imply that as a parent the best way to reduce risky behaviors is simply to know about them. By developing a close relationship with your child, you encourage your child to disclose their involvement in risky activity, and the more they are willing to disclose such information, the less likely they are to do it. These patterns actually begin in adolescence, where parental knowledge, facilitated by child self-disclosure, is already a robust predictor of less involvement in substance use and delinquent activity (Jacobson and Crockett 2000). The patterns found during adolescence clearly continue into emerging adulthood.

Unfortunately, not all parents have developed a close relationship with their child prior to emerging adulthood and, lacking clear knowledge of their college student's involvement in risky activity, may turn to more invasive forms of control, that invariably backfire and actually drive the child further away from the parent. Psychological control is one form of control parents may engage in at this time. Lacking day-to-day contact with their student, parents may resort to psychological manipulation as a way to get their child to comply with them (Abaied and Emond 2013). Studies have found psychological control negatively associated with developmental outcomes in college students. Scott and Mallinckrodt (2005) followed up a group of high-achieving high school girls who had expressed an interest in science and who had participated in a prestigious National Science Foundation-funded summer enrichment program. They found that these women's likelihood of persisting in a science-related major in college was predicted by their level of science self-efficacy, the belief that they were good at science. Science self-efficacy was predicted, in turn, by having a father who did not engage in psychologically controlling behaviors, such as love-withdrawal and guilt-induction. In another study, Abaied and Emond (2013) found that psychological control by parents led to passive and avoidant approaches to solving interpersonal problems, such as not thinking about the problem or just staying away from the situation. In the study by Urry, Nelson, and Padilla-Walker (2011) about predictors of parental knowledge, they found that psychological control by parents ironically led to *less* child self-disclosure and hence less parental knowledge, perhaps the opposite of what the parent had intended by their control attempts. In conclusion, psychological control seems related to a passive, avoidant approach to problem-solving by college students who stay away from challenges and withdraw from their relationship with their parent. Unlike psychological control, which is usually enacted within the context of a hostile, authoritarian parent–child relationship, helicopter parenting represents the misguided attempt of a well-meaning parent to aid their child with the challenges of college life. I turn now to a more detailed consideration of the meaning and implications of this parenting behavior.

Helicopter Parenting and College Adjustment

Helicopter parenting was popularized by the media to describe overprotective parents who have a hard time separating from their children and become overinvolved in their lives at college (Gabriel 2010; Marano 2010). Helicopter parenting may have come about because of cell phones and other forms of technology that have allowed parents to remain in almost constant contact with their children and to literally hover over them and survey their every move. According to some media reports, universities are instituting ceremonial rituals to help parents separate from their children when they drop them off at college and urging parents to remove themselves from campus as quickly as possible (Gabriel 2010).

Given the heightened concern by university administrators about the potentially problematic role of overprotective helicopter parents, the scientific community has begun to study the phenomena in recent years. Padilla-Walker and Nelson (2012) argued that helicopter parenting is distinguishable from both behavioral and psychological control, the two forms of control discussed previously. Helicopter parents are "highly invested, extremely concerned for the well-being of their children, and well-intentioned, albeit misdirected" (Padilla-Walker and Nelson 2012, 1178). These authors' five-item scale of helicopter parenting behaviors can be seen in Table 1.1, which I believe describes the phenomena more precisely than any more generalized characterization can do it justice.

Table 1.1 Helicopter parenting behaviors

1. My parent makes important decisions for me
2. My parent intervenes in settling disputes with my roommates or friends
3. My parent intervenes in solving problems with my employers or professors
4. My parent solves any crisis or problem I might have
5. My parent looks for jobs for me or tries to find other opportunities for me

Source: Items from a scale by Padilla-Walker and Nelson (2012).

Padilla-Walker and Nelson (2012) found that helicopter parenting was empirically distinguishable from behavioral and psychological control, although positively correlated with them, negatively correlated with autonomy encouragement (not surprisingly), and largely uncorrelated with parental warmth (meaning that you could be a relatively warm or cold helicopter parent). They also found that students reported an average of a 2 to a 2.14 on the 5-point scale for the level of helicopter parenting behaviors, which means that most students said their parents were *not* engaging in these behaviors. This should be kept in mind, when evaluating the media hype about the "crisis" of overinvolved parenting. Finally, Padilla-Walker and Nelson found that helicopter parenting was related to lower levels of school engagement by the students; it was unrelated to students' self-worth, identity achievement, or sense of being an adult.

Although Padilla-Walker and Nelson's results do not support the contention that helicopter parenting is a crisis within the current generation of college students, as contended by some media reports (Marano 2014), their findings do suggest that helicopter parenting is associated with a certain level of apathy and academic disengagement in students. Parallel results have been obtained in more recent scientific reports. Schiffrin et al. (2014) developed their own nine-item measure of helicopter parenting, which focused on similarly intrusive, overcontrolling parental behaviors, such as "my mother monitors my diet," or "If I were to receive a low grade that I felt was unfair, my mother would call the professor" (552), within a sample of 300 college undergraduates (over 85 percent female) at a mid-Atlantic public liberal arts college. Helicopter parenting was associated with greater depression and with less life satisfaction reported by the students and these effects were mediated by the students feeling less competent and less autonomous. It should be noted that students again reported a fairly low level of helicopter parenting within Schiffrin's sample as well (mean level of a 2.00 on a 7-point scale although with a range as a high as a 5.44), suggesting that these extreme parental controlling behaviors are not common, at least not as reported by students themselves.

Two very recent studies have added to the complexity of our understanding of the effects of helicopter parenting. Willoughby, Hersh, Padilla-Walker, and Nelson (2015) found that helicopter parenting was associated with students endorsing the belief that being single held advantages over being married and these students expected to get married at a later age. What is noteworthy about these findings is that a later expected age of marriage is associated with more sexual risk-taking behavior during the emerging adult college years and often with less stable, romantic relationships. Willoughby and colleagues interpret their results by suggesting that the over involvement by helicopter parents contributes to students feeling less freedom and thereby wanting to expand their marital horizons and remaining single for longer. Ironically, by seeking to over-control their children, these parents are actually exposing their children to greater risk, as a longer marital horizon contributes to riskier behaviors. Finally, Nelson, Padilla-Walker, and Nielson (2015) found that helicopter parenting, in the context of low parental warmth, was related to low self-worth and greater risky behaviors, such as drug use and shoplifting among college students, whereas helicopter parenting, within the context of high parental warmth, was unrelated to self-worth and actually related to fewer risky behaviors.

The general conclusion of these studies is that helicopter parenting is another form of parental control that is distinguishable from punitive forms of behavioral or psychological control but that is directed at controlling a child's choices and decisions within a college setting. Perhaps springing from a parent's lack of day-to-day access to their children, and from some sense of separation-anxiety on the part of the parent, helicopter parenting is nonetheless psychologically manipulative and intrusive and its effects are largely negative for students' development. The primary effects appear to be psychological, leaving the child feeling helpless and stifled. On the other hand, some level of helicopter parenting, in the context of a warm parent–child relationship, may prevent the child from engaging in some forms of risky behaviors.

Some Conclusions about Parenting College Students

If we look across the studies of parenting with college students, some broad conclusions can be drawn. It appears that college represents an important transitional moment in the parent–child relationship, where relational dynamics need to be re-fashioned. Whereas rational, child-centered control and limit-setting is the watch word of effective parenting with young and school-aged children, control is no longer the primary task of parenting college students. Rather parents need to believe that their college students are competent enough to make their own decisions and their role is to be a sound-boarding. Parents' knowledge of their college students' activities predicts their students' involvement in healthy activities and avoidance of high-risk behaviors. Parental knowledge is facilitated by student self-disclosure to the parent about their activities. In order for their student to tell them what is going on in their lives, the student needs to feel close to their parent and they need to feel like their parent will respect and listen to them without solving the problem for them (once the parent tells them how to solve the problem, they are acting like a helicopter parent). This is not an easy thing for a parent to do. It takes an act of courage on a parent's part that the student will be able to work through the problem largely on his or her own. But, it is the most effective way to help students solve problems during emerging adulthood. Of course, the parent–child relationship does not exist in a vacuum. Rather, it exists in the context of a larger family system, which can include a marital system, a step-family, and the sometimes uncomfortable dynamics of a recent or still painful divorce within the family. I turn now to examining the effects of larger family systems on college student adjustment.

Family Dynamics and College Adjustment

Beyond the parent–child relationship, other dynamics within the family affect students' adjustment to college. I will consider three issues:

(1) dysfunctional family systems; (2) marital discord; and (3) the effects of divorce and stepfamily formation on college adjustment.

According to family systems theory (Minuchin 1974), the family is organized into a series of subsystems, including the marital subsystem, the parent–child subsystem, and the sibling subsystem. Each of these subsystems is governed by a set of unwritten rules that dictate how much information should be shared across subsystems. In healthy families, subsystems have clear boundaries, regulating the flow of information across subsystems. As a good example, the marital subsystem should ensure that children are excluded from issues that are purely marital in nature, such as sexual issues or financial decision making within the family. In less healthy families, where marital conflict may be high and not well regulated by parents, the danger arises that children will become triangulated within their parents' conflict (Faber et al. 2003).

Fred Lopez developed the Family Structure Survey (FSS) to examine the existence of dysfunctional patterns of functioning within families with college students. The four subscales of FSS focused on (1) parent–child role reversal, (2) parent–child over involvement, (3) marital conflict, and (4) fear of separation. Lopez and his colleagues found that college students from more dysfunctional families reported greater difficulty with psychological separation from their parents and with academic and personal-emotional adjustment to college (Lopez, Campbell, and Watkins 1988). Interestingly, Lopez et al. found a different pattern of separation difficulties for male and female students who were caught up in dysfunctional family systems. The men showed a pattern of angry but distant relationship with their parents whereas the women showed a pattern of angry but dependent relationship with parents, suggesting that the parents were drawing their daughters into their ongoing conflicts.

In a second study, Lopez, Campbell, and Watkins (1989) reported that depressed college students were angrily involved with their parents and frequently became involved in inappropriate, boundary-crossing relationships with their parents, including high rates of parent–child role reversal, parent–child over involvement, and fear of separation. Interestingly, Lopez, Campbell, and Watkins found that marital conflict per se, without the presence of dysfunctional family dynamics, was not necessarily detrimental for students' psychological development. In families, where marital conflict occurred in the context of low levels of parent–child role reversal, parent–child over involvement, and fear of separation, students were able to show high levels of psychological separation from parents, although daughters still showed some angry, conflictual feelings toward their parents (Lopez, Campbell, and Watkins 1988). In a similar line of research, Faber et al. (2003) showed that rigid, cross-generational communication patterns, suggesting that children were being triangulated within an unhealthy parental coalition, were associated with a lack of identity exploration or commitment among college students; these students were more likely to be stuck at the diffused or moratorium stages of identity development rather than moving toward identity achievement. Interesting, spousal conflict per se was not related to identity status variables in Faber's study.

One of the legacies of family systems theory has been to highlight the very important role that marital relationships play in the healthy development of children across the lifespan. A fair amount of research has focused on the effects specifically of marital and household conflict on college adjustment. I turn next to that research.

The Effect of Marital Conflict on College Student Adjustment

Research has shown that students exposed to ongoing marital and household conflict report dissatisfaction with life and negative affect, whether they come from divorced or married households (Love and Murdock 2004). Moreover, and perhaps not surprisingly, students exposed to marital conflict have a difficult time forming satisfying romantic relationships in college (Cui and Fincham 2010). One question is what it is about marital conflict that is particularly distressing to college students.

In studies with children, researchers have shown that it is how they *appraise* the conflict that is most predictive of their reactions and adjustment to the conflict (Grych, Seid, and Fincham 1992). Children who feel threatened by the conflict and who blame themselves for their parents' fights are particularly at risk for negative outcomes. Research with college students has found that a high degree of threat perceptions were the most predictive of adjustment difficulties, in terms of depression, stress, and externalizing and internalizing symptoms, but this was particularly true for students from low income backgrounds, who may have experienced their parents' marital conflicts as particularly threatening of their financial well-being at college (since getting divorced may make it more likely that the student would have to drop out of college) (Lucas-Thompson and Hostinar 2013). Studies with college students have also found that self-blame for parents' marital conflict was related to more aggression and hostility and to down-regulation of the hypothalamic pituitary axis, suggesting a chronic stress condition (Lucas-Thompson and Hostinar 2013; Arshad and Naz 2014).

In addition to understanding how college students appraise their parents' conflict, researchers have examined the mechanisms by which marital conflict leads to negative adjustment outcomes for college students. Social learning theory suggests that students learn how to resolve problems in their own relationships by watching how their parents solved their own problems; they model and imitate their parents' conflict behaviors. Cui and Fincham (2010) found that parents' marital conflict predicted lower current romantic relationship quality and that conflict in one's current relationship fully mediated that effect, meaning that parents who engaged in conflictual behaviors modeled a type of fighting that was imitated by the students, which, in turn, resulted in the students experiencing a less good quality relationship with their romantic partner in college.

Another possible mechanism that may link marital conflict to students' social difficulties in college is that students may have bad feelings associated with growing up in a family filled with conflict and those negative feelings may interfere with students' ability to interact comfortably with peers. Rhoades and Wood (2014) hypothesized that students may find their negative emotions about their family distressing enough to lead them to feel anxious about social interactions with peers or to avoid peer interactions altogether. They found that family conflict, both marital and more general family conflict, was related to greater emotional distress about the family, which, in turn, was related to worse social adjustment, in terms of less social assertiveness, less dating competence, and less feelings of intimacy with a close friend or romantic partner.

The research reviewed so far on dysfunctional family systems and marital conflict has important implications for counselors working with college students in distress. First, counselors need to help students process what has happened in their families. The students need to learn how to separate themselves from their families, and especially from their parents' fights, and learn not to blame themselves or to get too overinvolved with their parents' conflicts. Also, counselors need to help college students learn skills to manage their family relationships more effectively, including preparing themselves psychologically when they return home for visits during a holiday or during breaks as these reunions may cause significant stress and anxiety for students who are returning to families where conflict is high and unresolved (Lopez, Campbell, and Watkins 1988; Lucas-Thompson and Hostinar 2013; Rhoades and Wood 2014). Although these recommendations are equally valid for students from intact and divorced or stepfamilies, additional challenges may exist if the student is dealing with a blended family.

Divorce, Stepfamilies, and College Adjustment

Divorce occurs in 51 percent of all marriages in the United States as of the latest statistics (Love and Murdock 2004), suggesting that many college students have experienced a divorce prior to or during the college transition. Given the ubiquity of the event, it is unlikely that divorce has uniformly negative effects on college student development or adjustment (Hannum and Dvorak 2004). In fact, Feenstra et al. (2001) found no relationship between family structure (i.e., coming from a divorced versus intact family background) and adjustment to college during the first year. It is known that divorce can reduce marital conflict and children who transition from a highly conflictual married household to a less conflictual divorced household may do better over time (Hannum and Dvorak 2004).

On the other hand, some studies have shown that college students from divorced households do struggle in college, especially in terms of their social adjustment and formation of romantic relationships. Hannum and Dvorak (2004) found, in a sample of first-year college students, that divorce when the student was 9 to 10 years old was associated not only with less family conflict but also with a less good attachment relationship with one's father. Additionally, divorce-status predicted more social adjustment difficulties (but not more psychological distress) even after controlling for the quality of the attachment relationship with one's father. Cui and Fincham (2010) found that students from divorced backgrounds reported lower quality romantic relationships. This link was mediated by two variables. Students from divorced backgrounds saw marriage as a less stable institution and expressed a lower level of commitment to their own current romantic relationship with their partner in college, which directly predicted lower relationship quality ratings. Cui and Fincham's results suggest that students from divorced backgrounds have less belief in the longevity of marriage, which, in turn, affects their ability to commit to a partner and form a satisfying intimate relationship.

Divorce often results in becoming part of a stepfamily or blended family. There is some research to suggest that children raised in stepfamilies may also struggle with more behavioral problems during the school years and may continue to have difficulties in college (Love and Murdock 2004). A possible mechanism here is the attachment relationship. Attachment may be disrupted in the stepfamily formation process because the trauma of divorce and re-marriage makes it harder for children to form stable attachment relationships with caregivers who may themselves be less available. In a diverse sample (50 percent ethnic minority) drawn from two community colleges and one university, Love and Murdock found that being part of a stepfamily predicted lower levels of father attachment (even in stepmother, biological father families) and somewhat lower levels of mother attachment (even in biological mother, stepfather families). Being part of a stepfamily also predicted more difficulty in college, in terms of less satisfaction with life, less positive, and more negative emotions, and these results held even after controlling for the significant effects of the level of conflict in the family. Disrupted attachment relationships served as one significant mediator of the effect of stepfamily status on psychological adjustment difficulties in college.

Conclusions Regarding Family Dynamics and College Adjustment

Students are affected by what goes on in their families as they make the transition to college. The more preoccupied they are by conflicts at home, the more involved they are in their parents' fights, the less likely they are able to concentrate on their studies, to feel good about school, and to form stable, positive, and intimate relationships with peers and romantic partners. If parents keep their marital conflicts sequestered from their college-aged children and are able to parent as a united team, then their students may do fine, although students are likely still to be aware of what is going on and may feel some anger or concern about their parents' relationship (especially daughters).

Students from divorced and stepfamily backgrounds, who are extremely common in the college environment, are mildly "at-risk," especially if there is still ongoing conflict between the divorced parents or within the step-parent families. The effects of divorce and marital conflict are most visible in the social relationships that students form with their close peer and romantic partners at school where, unfortunately, patterns of conflict management and levels of commitment to the relationship tend to get replicated. Students need to be encouraged to learn new ways to manage conflict in their romantic relationships and to believe that they can form more stable, committed relationships than perhaps their parents were able to—this will form the topic of subsequent chapters of this book on romantic relationships and intervention research with college students. For now, I turn to one other important formative adult relationship in the lives of college students, namely faculty–student relations.

The Effects of Faculty–Student Relationships on College Adjustment

Faculty represent a major socialization influence on the lives of young college students. Faculty model high achievement and encourage hard work and academic persistence, thereby upholding important values of most universities. Scholars of higher education argue that student interactions with faculty are key components of their feeling integrated into the campus community, learning to adopt the value system of the university, and thereby deciding to stay at the university, rather than drop out or transfer to another university (Pascarella and Terenzini 2005; Tinto 1993).

Pascarella and Terenzini completed a series of studies examining the impact of faculty–student interactions on college student adjustment. Using a sample of approximately 750 first-year students at Syracuse University, they examined the role of *informal* faculty–student interactions that occurred outside the classroom as predictors of academic and personal adjustment outcomes by the end of the first year of college. They showed that those students who reported more interactions with faculty members outside the classroom had higher GPAs by the end of the year, were more likely to persist at the university, and showed growth in both their intellectual and personal development, meaning that they could think more abstractly and critically evaluate concepts, had a better understanding of themselves, and had clearer career goals and plans (Pascarella and Terenzini 1977, 1978, 1980). Importantly, Pascarella and Terenzini controlled for a wide range of demographic and background characteristics in their analyses, including high school GPA, Scholastic Aptitude Test (SAT) scores, and parents' education level, suggesting that the gains associated with greater faculty–student interactions were not simply an artifact of already high-achieving students seeking out more faculty contact. Pascarella and Terenzini's initial work has been replicated in more recent studies, showing similar results linking frequent, high quality student–faculty interactions to gains in students' GPAs, academic persistence, and intellectual skill development (Kim and Sax 2014). Student–faculty interactions have also been related to several positive psychosocial outcomes in college, including greater college satisfaction, educational aspirations, academic self-concept, and racial tolerance (Kim and Sax 2009; Kim and Sax 2014; Kuh and Hu 2001).

Faculty can interact with students in a variety of ways, around a variety of topics. Pascarella and Terenzini emphasized informal interactions that occur outside the classroom. Within that context, they found that conversations between faculty and students, which focused on career concerns and intellectual matters, best predicted students' academic and personal development, whereas personal discussions were not related to students' adjustment outcomes. More recent research has suggested that the impact of informal faculty–student interactions may vary according to the type of major or field of study that students are involved in (Kim and Sax 2014). These researchers found that having been a guest at a professor's house had a differential impact on students' academic self-concept depending on whether the student was an arts, humanities, or social sciences major or a natural sciences, engineering, or business major. For arts and humanities majors, having been a guest at a professor's house was positively and significantly related to gains in academic self-concept from freshmen to senior year of college. Interestingly, having been a guest at a professor's house had no effect on student's academic self-concept if they were a natural sciences, engineering, or business major. The authors interpret their findings in light of the particular kinds of skills that faculty may be seeking to instill in their students across these different majors. Within the natural sciences and business fields, faculty may emphasize more heavily analytic and mathematical reasoning skills, presumably taught through classroom exercises and project-based learning, and a visit to a professor's home may do little to enhance this kind of experience. On the other hand, within the arts, humanities, and social sciences, faculty may seek to develop a mentor–protégé relationship with their students, fostering creativity and interpersonal skills, skills that may indeed be enhanced by visits to a professor's home. Overall, Kim and Sax found that students from the arts and humanities fields formed closer, more satisfying relationships with faculty than did students from natural science and business majors, supporting the importance of a mentor–protégé relationship within those fields of study.

Of course, faculty interact with students within the classroom as well and those interactions also significantly impact students' intellectual development. In the same study, Kim and Sax (2014) found that challenging a professor's ideas in class was the best predictor of gains in academic self-concept from freshmen to senior year of college and this effect was true for students of all majors, suggesting that open discussion of concepts in the classroom is valuable for academic self-development within all fields of study. Similarly, Bjorklund, Parente, and Sathianathan (2004) examined a large group of students participating in an innovative, design-driven introductory engineering class across the 19 campuses of the Penn State University system. These engineering courses were taught in small classes, using group-based projects, with students providing extensive evaluations of the quality of instructor interaction and feedback to students, the level of collaborative learning and peer climate, and gains made in classroom-related skills, such as problem-solving, occupational awareness, and engineering competence. Results showed that instructor interaction and feedback to students was the most consistent predictor of gains in all skill areas for these young engineering students, better than the level of collaborative learning, expected grade in the class, or SAT Math and Verbal scores. The interactive nature of these classes provided faculty many more opportunities to interact with their students than would be possible in a standard lecture-format classroom.

All researchers on faculty–student relationships agree that it is the quality of faculty–student interactions that matters more than the quantity. It is not just spending time with faculty inside or outside the classroom but rather really engaging with them in a meaningful interaction that facilitates a student's integration into the campus community. The challenge is how to make this happen. Research has shown that despite the high valuing of faculty–student interaction by university administrators and experts on higher education, it appears to happen quite infrequently. In a recent survey of close to 3,000 faculty across 45 institutions within the United States, faculty reported an average of about three substantive interactions outside of class per week across all their students during a typical academic term (Cox et al. 2010). In spite of this rather low number, there is variability in the frequency of faculty–student interactions, with some faculty reporting relatively higher rates of meaningful interactions with students than others. Given these findings, researchers have focused some attention on trying to understand what factors might help explain why some faculty have more interactions with students than others.

Factors that Predict Greater Likelihood of Faculty–Student Contact Outside of Class

Robert Wilson completed one of the first studies examining factors that affect the likelihood that faculty will have contact with their students outside the classroom (Wilson, Woods, and Gaff 1974). Wilson hypothesized that faculty would provide cues within the classroom of their level of social-psychological accessibility outside the classroom and those cues would predict how likely a student was to seek out that professor outside of class. Indeed, Wilson found that faculty who ran their classes in a particular way were the ones more likely to report substantive contact with students outside of class. These faculty structured their classes such that students were invited to help make class policies, they were encouraged to evaluate the course, and they were encouraged to express a viewpoint that differed from the faculty's views in the classroom. Additionally, these faculty differed in their evaluation practices, more likely to use essay-based exams and terms papers rather than "objective" testing, such as multiple-choice tests. Lest one conclude that Wilson's findings were the result of some kind of response-bias on the part of the faculty members, he found in follow-up studies these highly interactive faculty received the greatest number of nominations by graduating seniors as the teacher who "contributed most" to the student's personal or educational development and these faculty received the most nominations from their colleagues as "outstanding teachers" (Wilson, Woods, and Gaff 1974, 91).

Wilson's "social-psychological" accessibility hypothesis has had an enduring impact on the field of research on faculty–student interactions as it has intuitive appeal to it. It certainly makes sense that a faculty member who is open to students' viewpoints, who invites students to help structure and evaluate a class, is going to be seen as someone who is easy to talk to outside the classroom. In a recent attempt to replicate the accessibility hypothesis, Cox et al.'s (2010) survey of a large group of faculty across the United States found that in-classroom accessibility behaviors only explained about 9 to 11 percent of the variability in faculty members' casual and substantive interactions with students outside the classroom. Other factors that predicted greater contact with students included faculty choosing to teach as part of their professional role, the faculty member being a full-time member of the department, and their being nontenure-track. Clearly, simply having an interest in teaching and time devoted to it, without as much pressure to publish or engage in other university activities, tends to predict greater involvement with students outside the classroom.

Beyond institutional factors and faculty accessibility, psychologists have also considered the emotional qualities that may allow for quality faculty–student engagement. It is important to keep in mind that faculty–student interactions occur in the context of a relationship between two human beings who bring their own emotional strengths and weaknesses to the situation. To the extent that the faculty member and the student are emotionally ready for interaction, more high-quality interaction is likely to occur. On the faculty side, Lillis (2011–2012) showed that faculty who were high on emotional intelligence, meaning that they were good at recognizing their own feelings and the feelings of others and were able to demonstrate empathy, optimism, and leadership in working with others, had mentees who were less likely to indicate a desire to leave the university after one semester of a mentoring program than were students working with faculty of lower emotional intelligence. On the student side, Lopez (1997) showed that students form attachment representations of their professors. Students with a secure representation, meaning that they saw their professors as someone they could turn to and trust with personal information, were more likely to ask questions in class and to view their professors as competent and accessible. Lopez found further that secure representations of faculty were related to having had a secure attachment relationship with one's mother growing up—another example of Bowlby's concept of an internal working model being transferred from parental figures onto faculty figures. Interestingly, the idea of faculty members fulfilling surrogate parenting roles in the lives of college students has been pursued in thinking about the particular challenges of African American students adjusting to predominantly White institutions (PWIs), a line of inquiry I explore next.

Unique Challenges of African American Students Interacting with Faculty at Predominantly White Institutions

A number of studies have shown that African American students attending PWIs have less contact with faculty outside the classroom and are less academically integrated into the campus than their White counterparts (Guiffrida 2005; Nettles 1991). Moreover, African American students report lower rates of satisfaction in their contact with White faculty, in particular, at these institutions, finding them culturally insensitive to their needs, unapproachable, prone to generalizations about African American culture, and unrealistic models for their own success (Feagin, Vera, and Imani 1996; Guiffrida 2005). Although this evidence certainly points to the importance of universities hiring more African American faculty who can serve as useful role models to African American students, there may be other factors that could promote a more successful faculty–student relationship between African American students and both African American and White faculty members.

Guiffrida (2005) has conducted a rich, qualitative study examining the views of 19 high-achieving African American students attending a prestigious PWI on what makes a faculty member particularly "student-centered." Guiffrida conducted open-ended focus groups and individual interviews in which he asked these students about experiences that had aided and hindered their success at college. He did not ask them directly about faculty–student interactions; however, experiences with faculty members was a frequent theme of these students' comments. He found that these students valued faculty members who showed a sincere interest in them and who sometimes went "above and beyond the call of duty" to help them succeed at college. There were three characteristics that identified a faculty member as student-centered:

1. *Comprehensive career, academic, and personal advising*—Students described the faculty members as taking a holistic approach to advising and taking the time to listen to the students' "professional fears, dreams, and goals" (Guiffrida 2005, 708). The faculty member's advising went beyond meeting and listening to the student's concerns and included active monitoring of the student's progress in college. The faculty member would mandate regular meetings with the student even if the student had nothing to talk about and the student reported appreciating these meetings, even if they felt awkward at first.

2. *Support and advocacy*—African American students described the student-centered faculty at their university as going "above and beyond" by providing the student active forms of support and advocacy. Support could come in the form of helping the student locate money to stay in school, using personal contacts to help the student find employment in their chosen field, or even copying the reading materials for a student who could not afford the books for the class.

3. *Raising the bar: Believing in students and pushing them to succeed*—These faculty had particularly high expectations for the African American students in the classroom. This was particularly true for African American faculty working with African American students who communicated the message to these students that in order to overcome the burden of being a minority at a PWI, they had to

perform at a higher level to be perceived as equal to the White students at the university. The African American students in Guiffrida's study had mixed reactions to this experience of "raising the bar" on what was expected of them. For some, they saw it as another way in which faculty members took an active interest in the student's academic success and experienced it as additional motivation to do well. For others, they experienced it as another form of stereotyping that felt like a double standard and actually inhibited these students from doing well, by adding unneeded stress and anxiety to their academic experience.

The majority of the faculty members identified by students in Guiffrida's study who took on this expanded role with their students were African Americans themselves although occasionally a student would identify a White faculty member as carrying out some of these activities as well. Guiffrida notes that few in higher education would advocate for this kind of a comprehensive model toward faculty–student relationships and some might even see it as crossing professional boundaries. However, when viewed from a multicultural perspective, the behavior of the African American faculty toward African American students at this institution is very consistent with the educational concept known in the Black community as *othermothering*. Othermothering is a concept that originated in African American communities during slavery in which children, who were frequently orphaned by the sale or death of their mothers, were raised by othermothers, defined as "women who assist blood-mothers by sharing mothering responsibilities" (Collins 2000, 178, as quoted in Guiffrida 2005, 715). Eventually, othermothering became a theme of the educational practices of Black teachers in segregated school systems who would form kin-like relationships with their students, "visiting their homes to advocate for students, collaborate with their parents, and even tutor students and parents" (Guiffrida 2005, 716). This theme was carried on in Historically Black Colleges and Universities, where "… Black teacher trainees learned that it was their moral and spiritual obligation to uplift the Black community by attending not only to the students' academic development but also to their social and psychological development" (Guiffrida 2005, 716).

In conclusion, it appears that a highly nurturing, supportive, and demanding parental role, exercised by African American faculty at this institution was largely beneficial to the academic and personal development of these African American students. Guiffrida makes the point that not all faculty are going to be able to provide this kind of mentoring to African American students at their institutions. However, it is possible that a network of supportive resources and services can be set up by the larger university to provide more holistic, student-centered advising to African American students. Institutional offices such as multicultural centers, retention programs, and student-support programs could all be enlisted to provide some of the advising needs that African American students may not receive from their faculty mentors and advisors.

Conclusions Regarding Faculty–Student Relationships

The research reviewed in this section has highlighted the importance of faculty–student relationships for student's intellectual and personal development in college. Clearly, faculty are some of the most important adult figures that students interact with once in college and they often serve in surrogate parental roles. Evidence suggests that students value highly the kinds of interactions with faculty members that are good for their development. Grantham, Robinson, and Chapman (2015) conducted a qualitative analysis of students' submissions to a "Thank a Teacher" program in which students were invited to thank professors at North Carolina State University who had "gone beyond their standard roles and made a positive impact upon their lives" (Grantham, Robinson, and Chapman 2015, 126). Grantham et al. found that students were thankful to faculty for taking the time to discuss assignments and readings outside of class, to mentor them on their career plans, and to work with them on independent projects, exactly the kinds of activities that have been linked with gains in students' intellectual development in college. Students also expressed appreciation for faculty being caring and respectful in their interactions with them, for demonstrating enthusiasm in class, and for helping them to expand their worldview and opening their eyes to challenging topics. Clearly, students value faculty for their abilities to be emotionally present and intellectually stimulating as well.

As it happens, while writing this section of the book, I received an e-mail from a former student of mine, who happens to be an African American female, who expresses some of the same sentiments as those expressed by the students in Grantham et al.'s study. She has given me permission to quote her e-mail here:

> I am writing to you to thank you for investing in me during my time as a student in your class. Your class was very informative and engaging. Your class thoroughly prepared me to be able to complete graduate level work. This past semester, I completed my first semester in the Clinical Psychology masters program at X University. During the semester, I completed a Theories of Counseling & Psychotherapy class, and I felt so well equipped! From the tests, to the assignments you gave so many things you taught stuck with me. As I sat reflecting on my semester, I realized I owe you the utmost gratitude. Without you, and the hard work of my professor here at X, there is no way I could've received an A- in this class. It is my hope, to be able to come back to teach at X University one day, and give to other students who are interested in psychology the way you have given to me.
>
> —Diamond (Personal correspondence, January 15, 2016, quoted with permission from the student)

This student is able to reflect on what she learned from a class she took almost a year earlier and how she was able to apply that material to a graduate course on related material. She also felt a desire to express gratitude to her professor for teaching her well and expresses a desire to give back to others what she has gained. This student demonstrates personal and intellectual maturation that are the fruits of a successful college experience, presumably nurtured by the growth-promoting relationships she has experienced while in college. In the next chapter, I explore how personal relationships with close friends and romantic partners help shape students' college experiences as well.

CHAPTER 2

Students' Relationships with Roommates, Friends, and Romantic Partners in College

In the last chapter we explored the effect of students' relationships with parents and faculty on academic, social, and emotional adjustment to college. Beyond these important adult relationships, students invest much of their social resources during college in forming relationships with their peer groups and those relationships have a significant impact on their college adjustment as well as their growth from late adolescence into mature adulthood. The current chapter explores the impact of peer relationships on college adjustment and examines factors that predict success or failure in the formation of those relationships during college.

Roommate Relationships in College

What Makes Roommate Relationships Unique?

Most students transitioning to college and planning to live on campus are required to live with a roommate and, more often than not, it is someone they have never met before and with whom they have been randomly assigned to live (although more recently colleges have been using online matching systems to allow students to pick suitably matching roommates for their freshmen year, this system is not without its flaws, as will be discussed later in this section). Hence, roommate relationships are on the one hand involuntary and unchosen and yet, at the same time, there is the potential for great closeness, as roommates spend a tremendous amount of time together and need to negotiate shared living space (Gore, Cross, and Morris 2006; Hanasono and Nadler 2012). Hanasono and Nadler call roommate relationships a "special type of platonic friendship" (625) where, in addition to the elements of friendship such as closeness and sharing of personal information, there is also the need to create opportunities for privacy and a lack of interaction. All this, in the context of two individuals barely 18 years old who are transitioning from high school to college, living on their own for the first time, and exposed to the myriad challenges and opportunities of the college environment. It is no surprise that roommate relationships can significantly affect students' experience in college, both for good and for ill!

The Impact of Roommate Relationships on College Adjustment

Early studies showed that students' satisfaction with their living situations was associated with their emotional adjustment to college, their requests for room changes, perceptions of the university environment, and even their grade point average (GPA) (Gerst and Sweetwood 1973; Pace 1970; Waldo and Fuhrman 1981). Waldo (1984) found that roommates who reported a high-quality relationship and more positive communication with each other experienced less depression and fewer drinking problems. On the other hand, Dusselier et al. (2005) found that frequency of experiencing conflict with a roommate was a significant unique predictor of greater stress for students, even when controlling for many other interpersonal stressors, such as conflict with family, break up with a significant other, and conflict with faculty or staff on campus. Similarly, Lepore (1992) reported that roommate conflict increased over the course of a semester for pairs of new roommates moving into off-campus housing together and that these heightened levels of conflict predicted more psychological distress for these students, even when controlling for initial levels of distress experienced by the students. Importantly, however, Lepore found that roommates who could count on the support of their other friends did not experience an increase in psychological distress in the presence of increased roommate conflict, suggesting that friend support buffered the stress associated with roommate problems. Likewise, roommates buffered stress associated with friend conflicts, such that a good roommate relationship helped students not feel distressed about increasing conflicts they felt with their other friends over the course of the semester. Clearly, positive roommate relationships support social and emotional adjustment in college, whereas conflictual roommate interactions can increase stress and adjustment difficulties, especially when other supportive relationships are lacking.

Given that roommates live in close proximity and interact on a daily basis, they most likely influence each other's behavior as well, which can have both positive and negative effects on their college adjustment. Sacerdote (2001) found that one's roommate GPA in freshmen year of college was a significant predictor of one's own freshmen year GPA, after controlling for high school academic performance, drinking while in high school, and a number of dorm environmental variables, such as noise level or lighting conditions in the dorm. Roommate GPA did not influence participant's own GPA after freshmen year, presumably once the roommates no longer lived together. Also, roommates influenced each other with regard to deciding whether to join a fraternity or sorority or not but had no influence on each other's choice of majors in college. In a second study with a more diverse sample, Stinebrickner and Stinebrickner (2006) found that one's roommate's GPA in high school as well as one's roommate's family income level in high school predicted one's own academic performance during the first semester in college. Interestingly, this finding only applied to female college students who also spent considerably more time together than male roommates. Since the female roommates spent very limited time actually studying or working together, the authors speculate that the mechanism of influence here most likely is that the roommates are serving as good role models for each other to apply themselves to their academic pursuits.

Roommates do not only influence each other to do well in college, however. Researchers have also examined the ways in which they can model deviant and problematic behaviors for each other. Duncan et al. (2005) showed that male college students with a history of binge drinking in high school who were randomly assigned to live with a roommate who also had a history of binge drinking in high school were at significantly increased risk for binge drinking in college, almost four times more binge drinking episodes per month than if they were paired with a roommate who did not have a history of binge drinking. This effect was not present if the male student did not have a history of binge drinking himself nor was it present for female students, marijuana use, or for number of sexual partners. Duncan et al.'s (2005) results provide clear evidence for a "contagion" effect when it comes to male binge drinking, suggesting that campus personnel may want to consider this factor when deciding upon roommate assignments among male college students with a history of drinking behavior, especially given the problematic nature of binge drinking on college campuses, with over 50 percent of students considered binge drinkers (Wechsler et al. 2000).

Impact of Roommate Relationships on Changing Attitudes Toward Interracial Contact and Reducing Prejudice

Roommate relationships may also have an effect on students' attitudes and behaviors toward those of a different ethnic or racial background than themselves. Scientists who study prejudice have suggested that one of the best ways to reduce intergroup conflict is by having group members have contact with each other (Allport 1954; Pettigrew 1998). The success of this contact is predicated on the conditions that group members are of relatively equal status to each other and that they cooperate with each other toward achieving common goals (Shook and Fazio 2008b). From these conditions emerge intergroup friendships that strengthen the bonds between the groups and reduce prejudice that much further (Pettigrew 1998). As pointed out by Shook and Fazio (2008b), college roommates provide a real-life naturalistic experiment in which to explore how intergroup contact between individuals of equal status (two college roommates of different ethnic backgrounds) working toward a common goal (living together in relative equanimity in the same room) can build a friendship, learn to understand each other's worlds, and develop a greater sense of ease and comfort in interacting with other individuals who are of a different ethnic background than themselves.

The research on the effects of interracial roommate pairings on attitudes and behaviors toward those of a different ethnic background largely supports the contentions of the "contact" hypothesis spelled out earlier, although with the qualification that these roommate pairings result in satisfactory roommate relationships, which, unfortunately, is not always the case. Attitudinal studies have shown that White students randomly assigned to live with an African American roommate displayed more positive affect toward African Americans in general, less symbolic racism, and displayed more positivity on an implicit measure of racial attitudes (Shook and Fazio 2008a; Van Laar et al. 2005). In an innovative three-phase study of actual behavioral outcomes, Gaither and Sommers (2013) examined a group of White students who had been randomly assigned to live with either a White roommate or an "other-race" roommate (the other-race roommate could have been African American, Latino/a, or Asian-American). These students' previous intergroup contact and racial attitudes and experiences were assessed at Phase I, prior to coming to college. Phase II occurred four months later, mid-way through the first semester in college, at which point students answered questions concerning how much time they spent with their roommate, how happy they were with their roommate relationship, how many non-White friends they had, the strength of their own ethnic identity, and how much they had learned about other ethnic groups. Finally, Phase III of the study occurred the next semester, when the same students were invited into a laboratory situation in which they were asked to engage in a conversation with an African American student about the benefits and problems of affirmative action programs on college campuses. The students did not know that the laboratory procedure had anything to do with the original study regarding their roommate relationship and they did not know that the African American student they were interacting with was actually a member of the research team (a "confederate," to use the language of social psychological experimentation), posing as a fellow participant in the study.

Gaither and Sommers (2013) found that White students who had been randomly assigned to live with a non-White roommate reported a larger percentage of "other-race" friendships by Phase II of the study. They also had learned more about other ethnic groups and had a stronger sense of their own ethnic identity by mid-way through the first semester of college. They reported as much happiness and time spent with their roommate as those rooming with a White roommate. Finally, and most strikingly, during the laboratory procedure, the White students who had roomed with a non-White roommate reported feeling less anxious when interacting with the African American "student," feeling less of a need to explain themselves to this student, and engaging in fewer verbally controversial statements. Moreover, undergraduate coders who viewed videotapes of these students interacting with the African American confederate rated them as less anxious, more pleasant, smiling more often, and interacting in a generally more natural way than those students who had roomed with a White roommate their freshmen year. This study provides behavioral evidence that satisfactory interracial roommate relationships can promote not only more interracial contact and understanding but actually greater ease and comfort when interacting with someone of a different racial background than oneself.

The caveat here is that the roommate relationship needs to be positive in order to promote interracial understanding. Gaither and Sommers (2013) found that the White–non-White roommate pairs got along well and spent plenty of time together. Other studies have found that interracial roommates are sometimes less satisfying and more problematic than same-race roommate relationships and can result in higher rates of dissolution during the first semester of college (Shook and Fazio 2008b). In a large scale archival study of students attending a predominantly White college, Shook and Fazio (2008b) found that 15.1 percent of White-African American roommate pairs had dissolved by the end of the first semester compared with 8.1 percent of same-race White roommate relationships and 6.4 percent of same-race African American roommate relationships. Interestingly, these differences were only apparent when roommates had been randomly assigned to live together. When roommates had requested an interracial roommate, their rates of dissolution (6.1 percent) were no different than rates of dissolution for same-race White or African American pairs. As suggested by Shook and Fazio, these results highlight the importance of friendship (or the expectation of friendship) for the success of intergroup contact. Presumably, roommates who requested an interracial roommate expected to make friends with their roommate and this expectation led to a more successful relationship (in terms of lower dissolution rates) than when roommates were randomly paired together with no expectation of friendship. It is important to point out, however, that even with randomly assigned roommates, dissolution rates were relatively low, suggesting that most interracial roommate pairs were able to work out their differences in order to live together throughout the first semester of college, at least. These negotiation skills are critically important for students to be able to get along with a range of people in an increasingly diverse society. In the next section, I explore some of the skills and abilities students will need to develop in order to build a successful relationship with a roommate in college.

Factors that Predict Positive or Negative Roommate Relationships

Berg (1984) examined relational variables that predict whether previously unacquainted roommates would choose to continue to live together the following year. He found that roommates who felt like they were meeting each other's needs and made efforts to be helpful when help was most needed, reported a satisfying relationship the following semester and were more likely to report planning to continue living together compared with roommates who did not meet each other's needs. Additionally, Berg (1984) found that too much self-disclosure of personal information too early in the relationship led to less liking of one's roommate over time. Other researchers have found different results with regard to self-disclosure of personal information in the context of a close relationship.

According to these studies, self-disclosure is an important component of the formation of intimacy in a roommate relationship (Gore, Cross, and Morris 2006). Intimacy is defined as "an interpersonal process that involves communication of personal feelings and information to another person who responds warmly and sympathetically" (Reis and Shaver 1988, 375). The process begins by the first person disclosing emotionally relevant information about him or herself, thereby communicating trust and liking for his or her partner and a desire to build a relationship. Then, importantly, the partner needs to be responsive to the person's disclosures, showing understanding, validation, and caring for the shared information. In this way, intimacy is built.

Gore, Cross, and Morris (2006) examined pairs of roommates interacting over the course of a month and found that emotional self-disclosure by the first roommate led the second roommate to perceiving this roommate as emotionally responsive to personal self-disclosures, which, in turn, led roommate two to being satisfied with their relationship. The second roommate's satisfaction with the relationship then led to more personal self-disclosure by roommate two, leading the first roommate to perceiving roommate two as being emotionally responsive to self-disclosures and leading the first roommate to being satisfied with the relationship. Ultimately, the first roommate's satisfaction with the relationship led to another round of self-disclosure, continuing to broaden-and-build the intimacy between the roommates (see Figure 2.1 for a depiction of the results of this study).

There are a few important implications of this study. First, students who are more self-disclosing of their own personal lives are also perceived as more emotionally responsive to the disclosures of their roommates and it is this responsiveness that is particularly important in building satisfying relationships. Second, the process of intimacy formation is clearly cyclical, where one roommate's level of satisfaction in the relationship leads to greater self-disclosure by that roommate, which then leads, through the process of emotional responsiveness, to greater satisfaction on the part of the other roommate.

A final study specifically explored the individual, partner, and relational-dynamic factors that might help explain why roommate pairs decide to stay together versus split up after living together for one semester (Bahns et al. 2013). The study focused on 115 same-sex, freshmen roommate dyads who did not know each other before living together and who filled out questionnaires about themselves, about each other, and about qualities of their relationship, near the beginning of the semester and then again 10 weeks later. Bahns and colleagues found that the roommates' perceptions of their *own* mental health affected their desire to change roommates but not their perception of their roommate's mental health. Roommates who were more depressed, anxious, or lacking in trust desired to change roommates but it did not matter if they perceived their roommate as higher in these qualities. On the other hand, roommates did report that poor conflict resolution, lack of supportiveness, and lack of tolerance for each other were important determinants of their desire to change roommates at the end of semester. Finally, Bahns et al. (2013) found that roommates who were well matched on their level of competitiveness in academic achievement goals, meaning they were either highly competitive or not competitive, desired to stay together, whereas

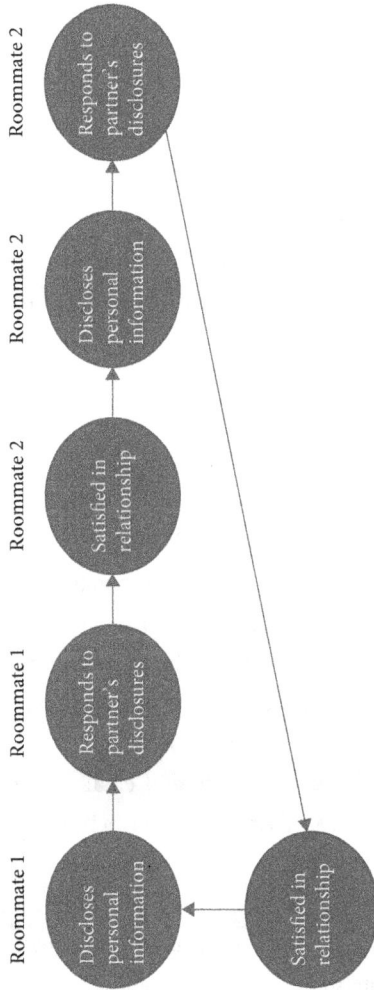

Figure 2.1 Links between self-disclosure, partner responsiveness, and relationship satisfaction in roommate relationships

Source: Adapted from Gore, Cross, and Martin (2006).

roommates who were mismatched, desired to change roommates by the end of semester.

Conclusions Regarding Roommate Relationships

Roommate relationships are important for the early life of college students. Roommate relationships teach students important communication skills, such as how to negotiate conflict, self-disclose appropriately, be responsive, and nurture and provide support when their partner is struggling with other relational disappointments. In fact, as will be reviewed in greater detail in Chapter 3, college counselors have designed intervention programs to enhance communication competencies among roommates, teaching them skills to listen better to their roommate's personal problems and to speak more competently with their roommate when they have a problem with them (Waldo 1989). These programs have shown considerable success for improving roommate relationship satisfaction and enhancing residence hall life in general.

Roommates also influence each other for good and for ill. They can not only help each other do well academically, modeling good study habits, but they can also model problematic drinking behavior, especially for those who enter college with a history of such behavior already. Finally, roommate relationships provide a rich environment in which students can learn to interact with someone who is different from themselves, ethnically, racially, in terms of abilities, learning styles, or even just in terms of socioeconomic background. For that to happen successfully, roommates need to be open to the experience and challenges that may arise and be given some help to negotiate differences between themselves and their roommates. In recent years, universities have been experimenting with a wide range of methodologies in which to assign roommates their freshmen year. From strict random assignment procedures, to matching systems using online matching programs, to allowing students to room with high school friends and even siblings, a wide range of programs and options exist (Foderaro 2010). Clearly, advantages and disadvantages exist for each option. Whatever assignment process is used, it would be wise for universities to consider what is gained and what is lost by allowing students to choose their roommates based on knowing them ahead of time, thereby missing out on the possibility of being exposed to someone different from yourself. Additionally, universities need to continue to offer residence hall intervention programs that assist roommates in learning the communication skills that will allow roommate relationships to flourish, no matter how well the roommates knew each other previously, as we know that those relationships are essential to a successful college transition.

Friendships in College

Theoretical Importance of Friendships for Emerging Adult Development

First off, it is important to note that developmental scholars locate the college years as a time when young people turn to friends to satisfy their most important emotional needs and use their friendships to advance their emerging understanding of themselves (Chickering and Reisser 1993; Erikson 1968; Trinke and Bartholomew 1997). Erikson described individuals of college age as in the Intimacy versus Isolation stage of development. Intimacy referred to close connections with a range of other people, from good friends to the burgeoning of romantic partnerships. Isolation was the danger associated with avoidance of contact with others but also served to protect young people from fusing with others and losing all sense of themselves, showing the strength of the drive toward intimacy during this time.

For Chickering, friendships and other student communities were "laboratories" in which students learned to "empathize, argue, and reflect" (Chickering and Reisser 1993, 392). Through open dialogue, often critiquing each other's ideas and challenging received wisdom, students advanced their understanding of themselves, clarified their values and goals, and developed their sense of purpose in college.

Finally, attachment researchers have examined the ways in which students shift seeking satisfaction of their most basic attachment needs from parents to peers during the emerging adult college transition (Markiewicz et al. 2006; Trinke and Bartholomew 1997). These researchers asked middle and high school, and college-aged students to identify the people who they are most likely to turn to, to satisfy three primary attachment-related needs: (1) *Proximity-seeking* ("Who is the person you most like to spend time with?"); (2) *Safe-haven* ("Who is the person who you most want to be with when you are feeling upset or down?"); and (3) *Secure-base* ("who is the person you feel will always be there for you?"). As students moved from middle to high school and then to college, best friends increasingly became the primary attachment figure to satisfy safe-haven needs whereas romantic partners, if the student had one, became the primary attachment figure for proximity-seeking and safe-haven needs. Interestingly, parents, particularly mothers, were still identified as the primary person to satisfy secure-base needs, even for college-aged students, suggesting that college students still believe (or want to believe) that their parents will always be there for them when they really need them, although they prefer to turn to their friends and romantic partners for advice and comfort most of the time!

Friendship Networks and College Student Adjustment

Networks of better friendship support predict college adjustment, especially during the initial transition to college but throughout the college experience as well. Hays and Oxley (1986) conducted a social network analysis, asking incoming freshmen during the 4th, 8th, and 12th week of their first semester to identify "all the people they had had contact with in the past three weeks" (306). They found that residential students reported more students as part of their social network, compared with commuters who tended to include parents and siblings more often as part of their network, and including students as part of your social network predicted better adjustment to college throughout the first term of college. Second, the size of one's social network as well as the percentage of interactions that occurred on campus predicted better adjustment to college, whereas the percentage that occurred at a workplace setting predicted worse adjustment. Finally, interactions aimed at "having fun" with one's social network were the best predictors of adjustment during the first term of college. These results highlight the importance of a rich network of on-campus social interactions in predicting adjustment during the initial transition to college.

Other researchers have examined the value of close friendships in predicting college adjustment during freshmen year. Pittman and Richmond (2008) found that changes in sense of belonging to campus over the course of one's freshmen year predicted greater competence and fewer internalizing behavior problems, whereas changes in positive friendship quality predicted fewer internalizing and externalizing behavior problems over time. The authors note that belonging to the campus is a subjective sense of being well liked and hence is more closely linked to other subjective measures of competence and internalizing distress, whereas reporting good quality friendships most likely involves a degree of social skills and social support that may help explain the link to fewer externalizing behavior problems as well. In either case, these results highlight the importance of fostering high-quality social relationships in helping students avoid behavioral difficulties as they transition to college and speak to the potential value of social-support based intervention programs that may help students build social skills and friendship networks (Mattanah et al. 2010; Pittman and Richmond 2008; Pratt et al. 2000).

A third study of friendship quality and college student development moves beyond freshmen year to examine the role that peers play in helping college students to explore their career options and make a commitment to a career trajectory (Felsman and Blustein 1999). These authors reasoned that close, mutual peer relationships help students feel comfortable exploring their career strengths and weaknesses, discussing their similarities and differences from each other, and thereby developing a greater understanding of what kinds of career possibilities interest them. Moreover, the security of close peer relationships provide students support as they begin to make tentative commitments to particular career trajectories. Felsman and Blustein (1999) found that students reporting more secure and intimate relationships with their friends also reported a greater willingness to explore career options and a greater sense of commitment to particular career choices, which includes an awareness of the obstacles to achieving career goals and a willingness to overcome those obstacles. Given that close friendships are important for college students' adjustment, it is important to determine what factors help explain how students form such friendships as they make the transition to college.

Factors Predicting Better Friendship Formation in College

A history of a secure attachment relationship to parents is an important predictor of students being able to form friendships in college and being able to rely on their friends as attachment figures (Parade, Leerkes, and Blankson 2010; Saferstein, Neimeyer, and Hagan 2005). Saferstein, Neimeyer, and Hagans (2005) found that students with a history of secure attachment reported greater companionship, greater sense of security, and less conflict in both their same-sex and their opposite-sex best friendships in college when compared with students who reported a history of either avoidant or anxious-ambivalent attachment. Similarly, in a short-term, longitudinal study across the first semester of college, Parade, Leerkes, and Blankson (2010) found that students who reported more secure attachment to their parents the summer prior to college had an easier time making friends during their first semester at college. Interestingly, Paredes et al. found that secure attachment to parents also predicted greater satisfaction with one's friendships but only for the ethnic minority participants in their study who were transitioning to a predominantly White institution. The authors reasoned that because of perceived racism at these institutions, ethnic minority students likely experience greater stress with the transition to college, which may have activated their attachment system and led them to rely more heavily on a secure attachment relationship with their parents to help them form satisfactory friendships with a new peer group.

In addition to the beneficial effects of positive, secure relationships with parents, a history of difficult family relationships can negatively impact a student's capacity to form close friendships in college (Green and King 2009). These authors examined the individual and combined effects of having parents who divorced and having been exposed to domestic violence while growing up (domestic violence was specifically defined in this study as having witnessed repeated incidents in which the student's father pushed, shoved, struck, punched, or threatened the student's mother with physical violence during an argument) on the qualities of the participants' best college friendship. Green and King (2009) found that the combination of having been exposed to domestic violence and having had their parents' divorce significantly adversely affected best friendships, leading these students to feel like their friends were less helpful to them, were less able to support them when they were feeling down, and generally seeing their friendships in a less favorable light. It seems that students who have been doubly traumatized by exposure to domestic violence leading to a divorce lose much capacity to form trusting relationships with close peers, ultimately forming friendships that are less intimate, supportive, and rewarding.

Unfortunately, students have little control over the factors I have reviewed thus far that affect their capacity to form friendships in college. However, they do have some control over how they express their emotions and this too has a significant impact on the formation of relationships in college (Graham et al. 2008). Although there is evidence that chronically depressed and angry individuals tend to be disliked by others (Segrin and Abramson 1994), Graham and his colleagues argue that appropriate expression of negative emotions is actually a healthy part of intimate relationships. Most people tend to express negative emotions, such as anger, sadness, or fear, only at certain times, when they are in need, directed at those who seemed interested, and this can help strengthen the relationship between friends. Graham et al. (2008) found that students who reported a greater willingness to express negative emotions also reported a larger social network, even after controlling for the students' level of extraversion. In a second study, students reported on their willingness to express negative emotions, the *summer* prior to coming to college. Then, 13 weeks into the first semester, the students reported on the quantity and quality of their social connections. Finally, Graham et al. were able to gather roommate reports of how much help and support the roommate had provided the target participant in the fall semester. Once again, Graham et al. (2008) found that willingness to express negative emotions, prior to coming to college, predicted a wider network of social connections, more satisfying social connections, and more support and encouragement from roommates, after controlling for these students' levels of neuroticism and self-esteem. Overall, these results provide support for the idea that appropriate expression of a range of emotions, rather than burdening others, helps strengthen and deepen social relationships and should be encouraged among college friendships. These results harken back to those on intimacy formation within roommate relationships, where appropriate emotional self-disclosure helps build intimate connections between close peer relationships. While forming new friendships in college is undoubtedly linked with better functioning, maintaining ties to high school friends is less unequivocally a predictor of positive adjustment in college. I turn now to a series of studies that have explored potential benefits and pitfalls associated with maintaining high school friendships during the transition to college.

Benefits and Pitfalls of Maintaining Relationships with High School Friends

It makes sense that high school students should prepare themselves for the transition to college by focusing on the new friendships they anticipate making at college. If they spend too much time preoccupied with thoughts of missing their high school friends and possibly losing those relationships forever, they are likely to have more difficulty with the college transition. Paul has termed this preoccupation "friendsickness" (Paul and Brier 2001; Paul and Kelleher 1995), a component of homesickness, but distinct from it, as it is focused specifically on the loss of one's friendship network, a loss that can feel more permanent than homesickness as the friendship network may never be re-created once a group of high school friends have graduated and moved away to college. Friendsickness is normative, in that all college students experience it to some degree, but too much may negatively impact adjustment during the transition to college. In a short-term longitudinal study during the first semester of college, Paul found that students who were most concerned about losing their friends over the summer reported the highest levels of friendsickness 10 weeks into the first semester of college. Friendsickness, in turn, predicted greater loneliness and worse self-esteem regarding being able to make and keep close friends in college. On the other hand, students who had reported focusing on making new friends at college during the summer assessment reported lower levels of friendsickness, less loneliness, and greater social self-esteem. These results support Paul's conceptualization of friendsickness as a type of self-fulfilling prophecy, in which the fear of losing high school friends and having difficulty making new friends in college results in a reality in college that matches those fearful expectations.

Although a preoccupation with losing high school friendships is certainly not adaptive to college adjustment, it is not clear whether students need to cut all ties with their high school friends in order to make a successful transition to college. Might maintaining some connections with their best friend from high school actually help college students during their first year and how easy is it to do this? Oswald and Clark (2003) examined those questions in a longitudinal study during the first year of college. Students completed questionnaires regarding the person they considered their "best friend" in high school during the first week of the fall semester and then again one month before the end of the spring semester. Oswald and Clark (2003) found that only 54 percent of the students reported that their best friends had remained "best" friends by the end of the year. Students found these friendships less rewarding and more costly to maintain with time and hence the students' level of investment and commitment to the relationship decreased as the year progressed. However, students who maintained regular contact with their best friend (via phone) experienced a high degree of satisfaction in the relationship and those students reported less loneliness in college, compared with students who reported maintaining a less close relationship with their best friend from high school.

The benefits and problems with maintaining contact with high schools friends have been explored in great detail in a study by Ranney and Troop-Gordon (2012), who examined computer-mediated forms of communication (CMCs) between college students and their friends from home, mid-way through the first semester of college (CMCs include e-mail and instant messaging via social networking sites but exclude any texting or voice-based communication). These authors were particularly interested in whether students communicate more frequently with friends from home when things are not going well with their friends in college and what impact these interactions with their distant friends have on their adjustment in college. They found that for students who were having difficulty with their friends in college, more communication with their friends at home predicted less depression and less anxiety over time in college. However, this was only true if the student reported that their relationship with their distant friends was of high quality. If they reported a lower quality or more conflictual relationship with their distant friends, they still engaged in a high rate of communication with those friends but the communication resulted in the student feeling more negative about their experiences in college. To a certain extent, the results of this study help reconcile and integrate the work on friendsickness by Paul and the findings regarding best friendships by Oswald and Clark. It appears that if students have a good relationship with their high school friends, maintaining some contact with them during the transition to college can provide much-needed social support, especially when the student is distressed about things not going well in their social relationships in college. On the other hand, troubled high school relationships have the potential to "draw" students back in, opening up a quagmire that is not easily resolved over the Internet but that the student has trouble letting go of. Ranney and Troop-Gordon (2012) advise college counselors to help these students "who may be embroiled in acrimonious distant friendships that compromise their emotional well-being and potentially their future college success" (858).

In the next section of this chapter, I explore the vicissitudes of college students' involvement in romantic relationships and discuss some of the ways in which students grow in their understanding of how to act romantically competent during this time period.

Romantic Relationships in College: A Map of the Territory

Students' sexual and romantic involvements in college vary widely, from fleeting physical encounters with no future contact to consistent sexual relationships with someone otherwise deemed a "friend," to enduring and committed romantic relationships. It is important to examine the characteristics of these different types of involvements prevalent on college campuses and determine some of the factors that influence how and why students get involved in these relationships.

Hooking Up

A common, and sometimes maladaptive, pattern of sexual involvement goes by the name "hooking up." As defined in the scholarly literature, a hookup is a "sexual interaction between partners who are not dating or in a romantic relationship and do not expect commitment" (Fielder, Carey, and Carey 2013, 637). A hookup is a deliberately vague term. The amount of physical interaction between partners during a hookup can vary greatly and it certainly need not necessarily include sexual intercourse. The key features of a hookup seem to be that the partners do not know each other well and there is no expectation of future contact. In that sense, a hookup is different from a first date or from sex with a friend and more reminiscent of what previous generations of young adults would have called a "one night stand" (Owen and Fincham 2011).

Hookups are prevalent on college campuses. Across a number of studies, prevalence rates range from 40 to 52 percent of students reporting having hooked up at least once within the past 12-month period in college (Fielder, Carey, and Carey 2013; Owen et al. 2010; Siebenbruner 2013). They are more common among Caucasian students, where 60 percent report having hooked up in a 12-month period, than among Asian-American (31 percent), African American (35 percent), or Hispanic (42.4 percent) students (Owens et al. 2010; see also Fielder, Carey, and Carey 2013). Hookups are more common at the beginning and the end of the semester than they are during the summer months, suggesting that just being in college around other peers is a trigger for hooking-up behavior (Fielder, Carey, and Carey 2013). Additionally, students from wealthier families and with more positive attitudes toward hooking up are more likely to hookup, whereas more religious students are less likely to hookup. Finally, alcohol use strongly predicts hookup behavior, especially sexual hookups, even more strongly for women than for men, perhaps by lowering women's inhibitions regarding societal sanctions against casual sexual behavior (Owens et al. 2010).

Friends with Benefits

Another type of casual sexual behavior common among college students is called "friends with benefits" (Puentes, Knox, and Zusman 2008; VanderDrift, Lehmiller, and Kelly 2012). As defined by VanderDrift, Lehmiller, and Kelly, friends with benefits relationships "are characterized as combining the psychological intimacy of a friendship with the physical intimacy of a romantic relationship, while avoiding the 'romantic' label" (2). Some friends with benefits were former romantic partners who ended their exclusive dating relationship but still engage in sexual encounters in the context of a "friendship," while others are friends who have added sex to their friendship without wishing to label their relationship a romantic partnership. Friends with benefits are sometimes "compromise relationships" by college students, in which they can have a somewhat serious relationship without the "drama" of a more significant, committed partnership (VanderDrift, Lehmiller, and Kelly 2012).

Limited research has been done on the prevalence or predictors of friends with benefits relationships among college students. Puentes, Knox, and Zusman (2008) found that approximately 50 percent of the students they surveyed said that they had been involved in a friends with benefits relationship at some point in their college career. Men, African American students, and more advanced students, were more likely to report friends with benefits relationships. Also, students who described themselves as hedonists, meaning that they pursue sex for the pleasure of it and not only in the context of a loving relationship, and who were realists, meaning they did not believe that there was only one true love for them, were more likely to have been involved in a friends with benefits relationship than students who were absolutists (no sex without a loving relationship) or romantic idealists. Taken together, these results suggest that friends with benefits relationships are common among individuals (i.e., hedonistic men) who may otherwise prize casual sexual behavior more generally.

Committed Romantic Partnerships

Students are also actively exploring serious romantic relationships while in college. In one close analysis of women's relational patterns across the first year of college, Fielder, Carey, and Carey (2013) found that during each month of college, 29 to 33 percent of women reported being in a romantic relationship as compared with 7 to 18 percent of women who reported a hookup encounter. Moreover, sexual intercourse was twice as common in the context of romantic partnerships as it was in the context of hookups for these women. Similarly, 75 percent of the women in another large-scale study of college students reported involvement in a romantic relationship and the modal number of romantic partners these women reported having in college was one (Siebenbruner 2013).

Students value romantic partnerships highly, which combine close friendship with sexual intimacy. One study asked students to write narrative accounts of what it meant to them to be involved in a romantic or sexual relationship with another person (Banker, Kaestle and Allen 2010). They found that students most highly valued relationships combining romantic and sexual intimacy in which there were "strong feelings," "deep emotional attachments," and "sexual commitments." Students saw these kinds of relationships as ideal, true love, and the most likely to last. They identified trust, commitment, and exclusivity as key elements of making these relationships successful. Although students idealized these types of relationships, frequently they did not think of themselves having that kind of a relationship and they were not sure that they could attain such a relationship. At times, students seemed to be settling for dead-end "sexual partnerships" because more idealized romantic relationships were unavailable or unattainable.

One reason these idealized romantic partnerships may be unavailable for students is because they feel like they are not ready to make such a commitment to another person, while they are still developing their identity and pursuing career-related goals (Shulman anjd Connolly 2013). In fact, students in romantic relationships in college often seek to strike a balance between intimacy and autonomy by developing unique relational living arrangements. One such arrangement that has received attention by researchers is called a "stayover relationship" (SO).

Stayover Relationships

A stayover relationship is defined as an arrangement in which "unmarried couples maintain a routine of overnight dates three or more nights per week while retaining separate residences" (Jamison and Ganong 2011, 537). Couples can stay over as often as six or seven nights a week and still be considered staying over, and not cohabiting, as long as they maintain separate residences. SO relationships are common among emerging adult college students. In a sample of 627 students, 65 percent said they had experienced an SO relationship at some point in college whereas only

15 percent said they had cohabited, which shows that these are distinct living arrangements (Jamison and Proulx 2013). Students report a number of advantages associated with SO relationships (Jamison and Ganong 2011). First, they enjoy sharing a bed with their partner, cuddling and snuggling, and waking up next to this person in the morning. Second, they report developing greater emotional closeness with their romantic partner by staying over. It is often in the late hours at each other's apartment or dorm room that their romantic partner will begin to open up and share personal information with them. Finally, staying over is a convenient way to see each other during their busy schedules of work, school, and internships. Sometimes, staying over was the only way to see their romantic partner at night.

At the same time, college students make efforts to keep SO relationships from leading into a cohabiting arrangement. They are clear to maintain separate residences and do not exchange keys with one another. They generally do not stay at the other person's place when their partner is not there and they feel comfortable asking the partner to leave for any reason, such as when they need to get work done or if they are having an argument. They are even careful not to leave personal belongings at each other's place, preferring instead to carry an overnight bag that they take with them for their "stay over" (Jamison and Ganong 2011).

When asked why they did not want the stay overs to turn into a cohabiting arrangement, the students said that they were not ready to make that kind of commitment to one another. Even though these were serious, long-term romantic relationships, students maintained a relatively short-term perspective about their relationships, not wanting them to get too serious at this point. They were concerned about balancing their relationship with other priorities in their life, such as career and educational goals, and did not want a commitment to a relational partner to get in the way of those goals. Learning to balance autonomy and intimacy within a serious romantic relationship is one of the most significant challenges facing college students during this time period. SOs appear to be a "stopgap measure" (550), a compromise arrangement, which allows for some level of commitment and intimacy in the context of a living situation that is intentionally limited.

Effects of Sexual and Romantic Relationship Involvement on College Adjustment

Effects of Hooking Up on Well-Being in College

Given the prevalence of hooking up among college students, it is unlikely that the experience is going to have uniformly positive or negative effects on students' functioning in college (Owen, Fincham, and Moore 2011). However, students' involvement in hookups do have an effect on their well-being and the research has shown that the effects are largely dependent on how students interpret the hooking up experience and subsequently react to it (Owen et al. 2010; Owen and Fincham 2011; Owen, Fincham, and Moore 2011; Strokoff, Owen, and Fincham 2015). First off, women are more likely to report a negative reaction to hooking up than men and use of alcohol during a hookup predicts less positive and more negative reactions to having hooked up the next day, especially among women, although across both genders as well (Owen et al. 2010; Owen and Fincham 2011). Importantly, in these studies, having a negative reaction to hooking up was associated with increased depression. On the other hand, women and men who hoped and discussed that the hookup might lead to a more committed relationship had a more positive reaction to the hookup the next day and less depression (Owen and Fincham 2011). It should be noted, however, that research has shown that as few as 20 percent of hookups lead to a committed relationship (Eisenberg et al. 2009), suggesting that these students' hopes for a committed relationship may provide short-term protection against negative reactions to having hooked up but are unlikely to be realized over the longer term.

The previously cited studies were cross-sectional, leaving open the question of whether students who are more depressed are more prone to getting involved in hookup relationships or whether hookup experiences actually lead to greater depression. A short-term longitudinal study by Owen et al. (2011) addressed this question. These authors studied college students over the course of one semester, whereby they measured depression and loneliness levels at the beginning and end of the semester and asked about history of hooking-up experiences at the beginning of the semester and then about subsequent hookups over the course of the semester. Owen et al. found that for students who were initially more depressed or more lonely, having a sexual hookup actually led to less depression and loneliness by the end of the semester, whereas for students who were initially not depressed or lonely, a sexual hookup led to more depression and loneliness. It is not entirely clear what explains these results but it may be that for fairly depressed and lonely students, a hookup represents some level of social engagement and connection that provides at least temporary relief of their depressive, isolative feelings in college. On the other hand, for students who are not depressed, a sexual hookup is not a particularly positive experience, and if they have a negative reaction to it, they experience some increased feelings of depression. In any case, as concluded by Owen and colleagues, "hooking up is not uniformly positive or negative in emerging adulthood in regards to psychological distress" (Owen, Fincham, and Moore 2011, 339).

Romantic Relationship Involvement and Well-Being in College

There is a long line of research showing that adults in marital relationships live longer and are better off physically and mentally when compared with adults who remain single throughout their adult lives (Coyne et al. 2001; Lillard and White 1995; Whisman and Kaiser 2008). Three specific mechanisms have been proposed to explain the link between marriage and better physical and mental health. First, individuals who marry are likely to be healthier physically and mentally to begin with, thereby better able to attract a mate. Second, marriage provides a tremendous amount of social support, where one's spouse is generally one's closest support person throughout life. Social support is a known predictor of better coping and outcomes across a range of physical and mental health stressors. Finally, the mechanism of behavioral regulation has been proposed as a means by which couples help keep each other healthy physically and mentally. Essentially, because couples are in daily contact with each other, and can monitor each other's behavior, they can provide important regulation over a range of potentially high-risk behaviors, such as excessive drinking, drug use, smoking, and unsafe driving practices (Braithwaite, Delevi, and Fincham 2010).

The question is whether these mechanisms apply equally well to dating relationships among college students and thereby whether those relationships are linked to better physical and mental health among students as well (Braithwaite, Delevi, and Fincham 2010; Whitton and Kuryluk 2012). First off, students have many other sources of social support besides their romantic partner and may not rely on their partner as heavily as spouses rely on each other for support. Second, because students are often not in daily contact, they may not be able to regulate each other's behavior to the same extent as spouses are able to do so. Finally, students are just beginning to develop their relationship skills and some research has shown that romantic relationships can be stressful for college students, actually leading to heightened levels of depression during the first year of college (Davila et al. 2004). For these reasons, a number of recent studies have further examined the associations between romantic relationship involvement and mental and physical well-being among college students.

Braithwaite, Delevi, and Fincham (2010) examined a large sample of single students versus those in a "committed, dating relationship" (4), asking about a range of physical and mental health symptoms. They also assessed these students' body mass index (BMI) and assessed engagement in risky behaviors, including number of sexual partners and frequency of alcohol, tobacco, and illicit drug use. They found that those in a committed relationship had better overall mental health, drank less often, had fewer sexual partners, and were less overweight. They found no effects for overall physical health and most of their effect sizes were very small, meaning that relationship status had a limited effect on well-being, as measured in this study. They also found that risky behaviors, especially drinking and number of sexual partners, mediated the effects of relationship status on mental health outcomes, which suggests that the benefits of being in a relationship on students' mental health were largely accounted for by the fact that these students were less likely to drink heavily and had fewer sexual partners (Braithwaite, Delevi, and Fincham 2010). Overall, these results provide modest support for the idea that a romantic relationship in college supports students' well-being and to the extent that it does so, it seems to do so primarily through the mechanism of behavioral regulation.

In a second study, Whitton et al. (2013) studied 889 college students who were in a romantic relationship or who were single and focused specifically on depression levels and problematic alcohol use. They found that women in committed relationships reported fewer depressive symptoms and less problematic drinking than single women. Men in committed relationships reported less problematic drinking but did not differ in depression levels from single men. These results support the idea that romantic relationships are beneficial to the mental health of women in particular, perhaps providing them a sense of support and social status in the community that protects against depressive symptomatology. For men, the benefits are clear in terms of behavioral regulation of problematic drinking, as was found by Braithwaite, Delevi, and Fincham (2010), but in terms of mental health, the results are less clear-cut. In fact, a second study by the same authors, found a similar result, showing that for men in long-term, committed romantic relationships, relationship satisfaction was related to less depression whereas for men in short-term relationships, their level of satisfaction was unrelated to their depression levels. For women in this study, level of relationship satisfaction predicted depression levels, regardless of relationship length (Whitton and Kuryluk 2012).

A final study of this topic advanced the earlier research by comparing college students who were in an exclusive romantic relationship with those who were single and those who were dating "multiple partners" across the first year of college (Salvatore, Kendler, and Dick 2014). Results suggested that students who were dating multiple partners during the first year of college, compared with both single students and those in an exclusive relationship, had elevated alcohol consumption and more alcohol problems by the end of their first year (these students did not show elevated alcohol problems at the beginning of college). These results suggest that it is not so much being in an exclusive relationship that protects young college students from risky behaviors but rather engaging with multiple relational partners that puts them at risk for increased alcohol consumption (not unlike results seen with hooking up reviewed earlier). Additionally, the study found that students who broke up with an exclusive partner during their first year also demonstrated elevated alcohol use by the end of their first year. This result is consistent with other research showing that relationship dissolution is associated with heavy drinking among emerging adult college students (Fleming et al. 2010). It could also be that experiencing a dissolution of one's relationship in college simply provided these students more opportunity to date multiple partners and drink more heavily as part of those dating experiences (Salvatore, Kendler, and Dick 2014).

Whether or not romantic relationships are clearly beneficial to students' mental health and well-being, they are definitely desired by college students and serve as a major topic of conversation among students, eliciting feelings of elation when things are going well, consternation, confusion, and even grief when not. In the final part of this section, I examine some recent research that has examined the concept of romantic competence, a construct that helps define what it means for a student to be able to function well in a romantic relationship and used to identify the skills needed for success in romantic relationships.

Romantic Competence in College Student Relationships

As they develop, children need to learn skills in order to interact competently with their playmates, peer groups, and developing friendships. Broadly speaking, these skills have been termed "social competencies" and research has focused on the development of children's social competence during early childhood and early adolescence (Buhrmester et al. 1988; Harter 1988). In a similar vein, researchers have argued that adolescents need to develop the competencies to be able to function adequately in a romantic relationship as well (Davila et al. 2009). An adolescent who is romantically competent knows how to successfully enter, maintain, and exit a romantic relationship, when needed. The skills associated with romantic competence begin in early adolescence, as teenagers explore romantic encounters in group dating contexts, but then grow and develop throughout adolescence and into emerging adulthood (Davila et al. 2009; Davila et al. in press; Kumar and Mattanah, in press).

In Davila's conceptualization of the construct, romantic competence involves the coordination of three interrelated skills. The three skills are defined and described in some detail as follows:

1. **Insight and learning**—Adolescents and emerging adults demonstrate an understanding of how relationships work, are reflective about their own experiences in relationships, and how their actions affect others in a relationship; they also demonstrate learning from past mistakes in relationships.
2. **Emotion regulation**—Adolescents and emerging adults are able to flexibly express a range of emotions in a relationship and to manage relational disappointments without becoming overly distraught or showing signs of extreme emotional dysregulation.
3. **Mutuality**—Adolescents and emerging adults are able to consider both their own needs and the needs of their partner in a relationship; they are neither overly self-sacrificing nor entitled in their approach to resolving disagreements and making decisions with their romantic partners.

Davila developed the romantic competence interview (RCI) to assess an individual's ability to thoughtfully reflect upon romantic relationship dilemmas and their own history of romantic and sexual intimacy, relationship conflict, and breakups they have experienced. At the end of the interview, the trained interviewer assesses the individual's answers across the entire interview in order to rate their level of insight, emotion regulation, mutuality, and general romantic competence, using a reliable coding system developed by Joanne Davila.

Davila's first study using the RCI focused on early adolescent girls (14 years old) and their mothers in which she was able to show that greater romantic competence in these girls was associated with more secure romantic attachment representations as well as greater marital satisfaction, as reported by the mothers. Importantly, girls who were more romantically competent demonstrated greater romantic involvement (having gone on a date, flirted with someone, kissed a date or romantic partner) but less sexual activity one year later (Davila et al. 2009). These results suggest that young girls who are more romantically competent demonstrate good judgment and decision making regarding their level of romantic involvement at this time period, exploring their romantic world through dates and mild forms of physical touching but avoiding early sexual intimacy, a known predictor of negative psychosocial outcomes for early adolescents (Welsh, Grello, and Harper 2003).

More recently, Davila and I have been studying the correlates of romantic competence among college students. We adapted the RCI for this age group, updating the questions to be age-appropriate but keeping the same basic format and coding system as was used with the early adolescents. Across three studies, including both men and women, we found that romantic competence is associated with greater relationship satisfaction and with fewer symptoms of depression and anxiety among emerging adults in a romantic relationship. Also, those students who are more romantically competent are better at recognizing the warning signs of a bad relationship and deciding to get out of a relationship when it is not going well, which are particularly important skills for emerging adults who are exploring their relational lives and not ready to make firm commitments. Finally, we have found that students who have a more secure attachment relationship with their parents and feel that their parents are less likely to intrude into their personal lives demonstrate greater skills on the romantic competence interview (Davila et al. in press; Kumar and Mattanah, in press).

Collectively, these results suggest that romantic competence is a useful way of describing the skills needed by college students to navigate the tricky waters of their romantic involvements—how to learn from their past mistakes, gain insights about relationships, manage their emotions in close relationships, and demonstrate mutuality with a romantic partner— ultimately, how to coordinate their thoughts, feelings, and behaviors regarding their romantic lives. Clearly, these skills lead to more successful relationships and to better decision making for both adolescents and emerging adults. Even more importantly, these skills can be taught. This will form part of the subject matter of Chapter 3 where I explore interventions designed to build relationship skills in college students. For now, I turn to one last aspect of the social life of college students, namely their involvement in larger social organizations in college, such as clubs and Greek life, and what impact their involvement in those organizations have on their adjustment.

Clubs and Social Organizations on College Campuses: Harmful or Helpful?

In addition to the individual relationships that students form at college, they also encounter other peers through their involvement in a myriad of social organizations during their college careers. Higher education experts, such as Arthur Chickering, view these student communities as critical for development in college (Chickering and Reisser 1993). Chickering argues that involvement in these organizations helps students to clarify their own values, sometimes by resisting the values of the group, or sometimes by joining the group in resisting the values of the larger institution, such as when a school newspaper sniffs out a scandal occurring within the university administration (Chickering and Reisser 1993). In order for a student community to optimally foster development, Chickering suggests that the following characteristics must be present:

1. The organization encourages regular interaction among its members.
2. The organization provides opportunities for collaborative projects.
3. The organization is small enough so that all voices are heard.
4. The organization includes individuals of diverse backgrounds.
5. The organization has boundaries of who is in and out and norms exist of what is considered acceptable behavior (Chickering and Reisser 1993, 398–99).

Unfortunately, not all student organizations exhibit these characteristics. This is where the controversy arises as to whether student organizations do more harm or good in fostering optimal student development and adjustment outcomes. Nowhere is this controversy more apparent than with regard to Greek life on college campuses (DeBard and Sacks 2011–2012; Hevel et al. 2015). Nationally, approximately 10 to 12 percent of college students are members of a fraternity or sorority during their undergraduate years (Debard and Sacks 2011–2012). According to the mission statement of most Greek organizations, these communities exist in order to foster a high level of scholarship, service, and integrity among its members in order to promote excellence in undergraduate education (just as one example, the mission statement of Sigma Chi, a well-respected national Fraternity, states: "The fundamental purpose of the Sigma Chi Fraternity is the cultivation, maintenance and accomplishment of the ideals of Friendship, Justice and Learning within our membership"—www.sigmachi.org/about). Ironically, Greek life members have been portrayed in the media as anything but highly scholarly and service-oriented. Rather, they are seen as anti-intellectual, often valorizing a culture of heavy drinking and promiscuous sexual behavior, and in some of the most virulent critiques, Greek life has been implicated in the promotion of a culture of rape on college campuses (Thériault 2015).

Given the controversy surrounding the image of Greek organizations, it is important to review the scholarly research that has examined the effects of participation in a Greek organization on student's adjustment and development in college. I focus on three recently completed and well-respected studies in this area. First, Glindemann and Geller (2003) examined whether excessive drinking is encouraged by fraternity parties or whether members of fraternities drink more heavily than nonfraternity members. They measured the blood-alcohol (BAC) level of 1,525 students attending 19 different weekend parties, 11 at a fraternity house and 8 at a private apartment. All parties were held on a Friday or Saturday evening and BAC levels were taken using breathalyzers between 11:30 p.m. and 12:30 a.m. from random, consenting students. Results showed that BAC levels were significantly higher among students attending fraternity parties when compared with students attending private apartment parties. Interestingly, students who were members of Greek life did not drink more heavily than those who were not part of Greek life, either at a fraternity party or at a private house party. These results suggest that it is the context of a fraternity party that is particularly conducive to excessive drinking, for anyone in attendance, more so than just being a member of a Greek organization per se.

A second study focused specifically on the academic performance and retention rates of students joining a Greek organization during their first year of college (DeBard and Sacks 2011–2012). This study analyzed data from 17 institutions across the United States, including both public and private institutions, a total of 6,115 students who joined a Greek organization and 39,983 not-affiliated students. The results of this study, summarized in Table 2.1, show that students who joined a Greek organization

Table 2.1 *Effects of joining a Greek organization in the fall or spring of freshmen year on grades, credits hours earned, and retention*

	Independents	Greeks (Fall)	Greeks (Spring)
GPA	2.96	3.04	3.17
Credit hours earned	28.53	27.68	32.27
Retention rates	0.86	0.93	0.97

Source: Data from Debard and Sacks (2011–2012).

Note: The differences between the groups were statistically significant such that Greeks (especially those that deferred membership to spring semester) earned higher GPAs, more credit hours in school, and were retained at higher rates. Also, these differences controlled for preexisting differences between the groups on high school American College Testing (ACT) scores.

in their freshmen year earned higher GPAs, more credit hours, and were more likely to stay at the university, compared with students who did not join a Greek organization. It should be noted that these results held up, even when controlling for pre-existing differences in these students' levels of academic achievement prior to coming to college, meaning that these results are not just a function of higher achieving students being more likely to join a Greek organization. This study is one of the few to find an academic advantage for students who are part of Greek organizations; however, the finding that students who join Greek organizations are more likely to remain at the university has been reported in a number of other studies (see Hevel et al. 2015 for further details). It is likely that membership in Greek organizations helps students feel integrated into the campus community, which is an important predictor of students' staying at a university rather than transferring to another institution or dropping out (Tinto 1993).

Hevel et al. (2015) found that for Caucasian students, membership in Greek organizations led to decreases in critical thinking skills over four years at college whereas for minority students, membership led to slight increases in critical thinking skills. Conversely, for minority students, membership in Greek organizations led to decreases in moral reasoning whereas for Caucasian students, membership led to increases in moral reasoning over time. Finally, these authors found that for students with lower levels of critical thinking skills coming into college, membership in Greek organizations led to decreases in critical thinking skills over time whereas for students high in positive attitudes toward lifelong learning, membership in a Greek organization led to increases in those positive attitudes over time. These results are complex but support previous research that has shown that Greek life can dampen critical thinking skills for Caucasian students (Pascarella et al. 1996) and negatively affect moral reasoning, in this case for minority students (Kilgannon and Erwin 1992). Also, they suggest that Greek life may enhance academic outcomes for already high achieving students but may encourage less talented students to turn away from academic pursuits (Hevel et al. 2015). Ultimately, results of this and similar studies have led experts on higher education to question the many resources, financial and institutional, that are devoted to Greek life on college campuses, given its limited effects on enhancing the moral or intellectual development of students (Hevel et al. 2015; Park 2014).

Beyond Greek life, researchers have been interested in the role of other student organizations in promoting the moral and civic life of students on college campuses. One study, in particular, focused on how students' involvement in a variety of campus organizations was related to their development of interracial friendships (Park 2014). Consistent with Chickering's earlier cited criteria of a student community that effectively promotes value development, Park reasoned that student organizations that encourage diverse groups of students to work together toward a common goal (such as an arts organization or a team sport) should effectively promote interracial friendships to a greater extent than student organizations that are racially homogenous and that espouse singular ideologies, ignoring inherent differences between group members. Park examined this question drawing from a racially diverse group of students participating in the National Longitudinal Study of Freshmen, a four-year longitudinal study conducted by Princeton University focused on 28 selective institutions. Park assessed students' involvement in a wide range of organizations, including Greek organizations, service organizations, career-related organizations, religious groups, musical or theater or arts groups, ethnic groups, and sports organizations.

Overall, Park found that Caucasian students were the least likely to have an interracial friend and they were the most likely to participate in Greek organizations, which was a highly racially isolating experience. Religious organizations were the most ethnically homogenous experience for Asian-American and African American students. Service, career, arts, and sports organizations were not particularly racially homogenous, especially not for students of color. Consistent with these patterns, Park found that being a member of a fraternity, a sorority, or a religious organization predicted less likelihood of having an interracial friendship in college, whereas having a more diverse group of friends in high school and being in a more diverse college environment made it more likely that one would have an interracial friendship. Being a member of other organizations was unrelated to forming interracial friendships.

Although Park (2014) questions the value of Greek life, given the ways in which it further isolates Caucasian students from interracial experiences in college, she does not recommend disbanding religious organizations, which can provide much needed moral support for ethnic minority students facing prejudice on college campuses. She does recommend, however, that campus ministry be encouraged to enter into dialogue with other campus personnel to promote interracial exchanges and interactions, hopefully helping to promote greater inclusiveness within these organizations. As far as other social organizations are concerned, they neither promoted nor interfered with students' development of interracial friendships although their diverse nature certainly provided opportunities for interaction. Park suggests that these organizations strive to promote tighter bonds among their members, perhaps partnering with residence halls or other campus organizations, thereby enhancing the possibilities for interracial friendships to form.

Conclusions

Chapter 2 has covered a lot of ground, from exploring the interpersonal dynamics that predict successful roommate relationships to describing the types of sexual entanglements college students find themselves in, to examining some of the benefits and pitfalls of social organizations on college campuses. There are two overarching conclusions that can be drawn from much of the research reviewed in this chapter, cutting across different kinds of peer relationships that students encounter in college. First, the quality of these relationships *matter* for how students function and succeed in college. A student who is happy with his or her roommate, who has good friends he or she can count for support, who is able to form a satisfying intimate relationship with a romantic partner, and who joins social organizations that stimulate and challenge him or her, is going to do better in college, not only socially and emotionally, but also academically, in terms of better grades, persistence, and more timely graduation from college. Second, developing high quality relationships is a challenging task for college students. Roommate relationships take work to succeed, as do friendships, as do romantic partnerships, and even the most socially skilled students can use help at times in navigating their social relationships. In recent years, a number of programs have been developed to assist students on college campuses to enhance their social and romantic competencies in order to function better in their close relationships. The last chapter of this book provides an introduction to some of those programs that hold promise in enhancing students' competence and adjustment to college.

CHAPTER 3

Interventions to Promote Relationship Functioning and Adjustment Outcomes Among College Students

The past chapters of this book have explored the role of significant inter-personal relationships in predicting student adjustment outcomes. In the current chapter, I examine what can be done to help students do better in college. Traditional ways of helping focus on counseling individual students who have been identified with particular mental health problems. A number of good books have been written on how to work with students from a counseling center perspective (Degges-White and Borzumato-Gainey 2014). However, there are significant limitations to this approach. First, it is likely to fail to reach a large cross-section of students who may be hesitant to seek counseling due to personal, structural, or cultural barriers to treatment (Conley, Travers, and Bryant 2013). Students may not think of themselves as having a "problem" or they may not wish to seek counseling because of the stigma associated with mental health services. Additionally, many students of color may not seek counseling because psychotherapy is not a traditional form of healing within their cultural background. As it turns out, college counseling centers are paradoxically both overburdened by the number of students seeking counseling services (Erdur-Baker et al. 2006) while at the same time underutilized by the general population of college students, where only about 10 percent of students who are experiencing significant symptoms of distress seek services (Conley, Travers, and Bryant 2013).

Taken together, these factors suggest that there is an important role for primary prevention interventions in helping students adjust better to college and preventing the development of problems in the first place. Primary prevention is a term used by community psychologists to refer to interventions that target wide groups of people, not necessarily diagnosed with a condition, but who can benefit from health promotion. Primary prevention contrasts with secondary or tertiary interventions targeting individuals already at risk for a problem or diagnosed with a problem, where help is needed to prevent further deterioration of the condition. Primary interventions with college students tend to work with small groups of students at a time, often in the context of a class or in "break out" sessions; they are usually facilitated by paraprofessionals, often more advanced students themselves at the university; they are targeted at the general population of students who are not identified as having a problem per se; and they focus on teaching a range of life management and social skills that have the potential to enhance students' mental well-being as well as promote their functioning across a range of relationships in college. Hence, these interventions hold promise for reaching a wide cross-section of students on college campuses, while providing them a de-stigmatized, low-cost program that can significantly enhance their personal and relational well-being. Importantly, these interventions needed to be evaluated empirically to determine their effectiveness. The current chapter examines a number of the most well-researched intervention programs that have been developed. I begin by reviewing a very recent meta-analysis that has examined the general effectiveness of primary prevention intervention programs with college students.

Does Primary Prevention Work with College Students?

In a recent meta-analysis, Conley, Durlak and Kirsch (2015) examined the overall effectiveness of primary prevention interventions with college undergraduates. These interventions were short term, lasting 10 hours or less; they were delivered in a group format, usually as part of college course or as a small group intervention; they focused on students across all four years of undergraduate education (some even focused on graduate students) and students had no preexisting mental health problems; and they used a wide variety of treatment techniques and strategies, the most common of which were cognitive-behavioral strategies, psychoeducation, relaxation, meditation, and mindfulness.

Across 103 studies, Conley, Durlak, and Kirsch (2015) found that preventative interventions were effective in ameliorating distressful symptoms. Students' distress went down to a significant degree from pre-intervention to post-intervention with an effect size about as large as what has been found when treating clients with individual therapy for an anxiety disorder. Conley et al. comment that the effect size they found is comparable or larger than most other preventative intervention studies conducted with school-age children or adolescents, suggesting that college students are prime targets for this work.

Interestingly, when examining specific treatment techniques, these researchers found that teaching specific skills such as mindfulness and cognitive modification of dysfunctional thoughts, and then providing opportunities for the students to practice those skills as part of the group and receive feedback on their performance of the skills, was particularly helpful in promoting better outcomes, when compared with just educating students about useful coping mechanisms without providing them opportunities to practice the skills in the group itself. This finding shows the potential value of group interventions in promoting change by providing students important input and feedback about their behavior.

A Social Support Intervention to Ease the Transition to College

One of the most stressful aspects of the transition to college is the disruption of a student's network of social support. Students graduating from high school and leaving home for college are expected to say goodbye to their high school friends, teachers, and neighbors, lessen their dependency on their family and make the transition to an entirely new set of peers and adult mentors and teachers in college, all in the space of a few months. This transition is stressful and many students don't make it, as we know that the first few weeks of the college transition are critical to long-term college adjustment and the decision to stay at the university or not (Pratt et al. 2000). Mindful of this stressful transition, universities normally offer orientation programs, usually lasting a long weekend or perhaps a week before school begins, to help entering students transition into college life, meet new students, and orient to the university. These orientation programs are helpful but they do little to bridge the gap in the student's social support network that will likely last for at least the first four to six weeks of college life, before more solid roommate and friendship relationships can be formed at college.

The "Bridge Over Troubled Water" social support intervention program (also called Transition to University or T2U Intervention Program) was designed specifically to bridge that gap, providing students an opportunity to discuss and normalize the college transition and to build a social support network, during the initial transition to college period (Ames et al. 2011; Mattanah et al. 2010; Pratt et al. 2000). The structure of this program is straightforward. Students meet in groups of about seven to nine students per group, co-facilitated by two advanced undergraduate students, for nine sessions, beginning soon after the semester begins. The first seven sessions are held during the first seven weeks of the Fall semester and the last two sessions are held in the Spring semester, as follow-up and wrap-up sessions. The facilitators can be thought of as "fellow journeyers" (Mattanah et al. 2010, 105) rather than as experts, since they went through the same experiences of the first-year students just a few years ago and often have wisdom and insight to share regarding the process of coping with college adjustment (Mattanah et al. 2010).

The intervention has a semi-structured curriculum that focuses on several key issues. Each includes a five-minute check-in portion, a 30-minute exercise in which students practice skills such as social initiation and resisting peer pressure, followed by a general discussion, and a wrap-up session. As seen in Table 3.1, the topics of the group sessions are highly salient for first-year students, such as developing a new network of social connections, learning how to balance social life with academic work, dealing with peer pressure in college, letting go of old social connections (especially after visiting home for Thanksgiving), and dealing with academic expectations and reality in college.

This intervention program has been rigorously evaluated in three different studies across four universities, two in Canada and two in the United States, with diverse campus communities. Results showed that those participating in the intervention, compared with control participants not provided any intervention, reported better overall adjustment to the campus (Pratt et al. 2000) and fewer symptoms of loneliness by the time the intervention was over in the Spring semester of their freshmen

Table 3.1 Issues of focus in the transition to university social support intervention program

1. Creating new social connections in college
2. Balancing school work and social life
3. Managing peer pressure and developing one's personal values
4. Saying goodbye to old social connections (after the Thanksgiving home visit)
5. Managing academic expectations and reality
6. Planning living situations for sophomore year
7. Processing feelings about group ending and saying goodbye

Source: Adapted from Pratt et al. (2000).

year (Mattanah et al. 2010). Moreover, students participating in the intervention also reaped academic benefits, missing fewer classes (Pratt et al. 2010) and demonstrating higher grade point averages the semester after the study was over (Mattanah et al. 2012). Mattanah et al. attributed their results to the fact that students in the intervention were less lonely, which, in turn, predicted greater academic performance the following semester, supporting the idea that a student's social and emotional adjustment to campus has an effect on their academic performance over time.

In conclusion, this social support-based intervention program is a low-cost, relatively easily administered intervention program that could become part of what colleges routinely offer to help students transition to college. One small campus in North Carolina, Queens University of Charlotte, has already begun doing so, offering the intervention program to about one-third of its entering class of first-year students, every year, for the past eight years. Students learn about the program during freshmen orientation and through tables set up around campus during the first week of classes and volunteer to participate in the program to fulfill one of their core curriculum requirements. Sessions run throughout the Fall and Spring semester of the students' first year, facilitated by upperclassmen, covering a wide range of topics, from college expectations, to bullying on campus, to dealing with romantic relationships concerns on Valentine's Day (Harper and Allegretti, personal communication, April 25, 2016). The university has found this program to be extremely helpful to its first-year students, improving their social and emotional experience on campus, and most importantly, enhancing retention rates, from second to third semester of college (Harper and Allegretti 2009; Harper and Allegretti 2013). Although the T2U program is very promising for facilitating the college transition, it does not specifically target relationship enhancement. The next set of interventions has been developed specifically to help students manage their relationships more effectively within the college environment.

Relationship Enhancement Interventions with College Students

Relationship Enhancement for College Roommates

Good roommate relationships aid students with their relational difficulties with other friends and romantic partners, whereas negative roommate interactions can exacerbate stress and depression levels during the college transition. Given these findings, a viable way to prevent symptoms and promote mental well-being among college students is to enhance relational competencies among college roommates (Waldo 1989).

Waldo developed a relationship enhancement program that was implemented by paraprofessional resident hall assistants (RAs) in small group workshops within students' residential living spaces (Waldo 1985; Waldo 1989). The groups of 8 to 14 students met for four 2-hour sessions in which very specific communication skills were taught and demonstrated. The skills focused on were: nonverbal communication, self-expression, demonstrating understanding, feedback, confrontation, and conflict resolution. For each skill, the leaders of the group first described and demonstrated the skill, then the students practiced the skill while being coached by the leaders, and finally the group members discussed their reactions to practicing the skill.

Using a randomized, waitlist-control design, Waldo (1989) tested whether this relationship enhancement program facilitated improved communication skills among roommates. In order to assess outcomes, he had participants complete a verbal task in which they wrote down what they would say to their roommate in response to situations in which they were listening to their roommate discuss a person problem, listening to their roommate discuss a conflict they had with them, speaking to their roommate about a personal problem of their own, and speaking to their roommate about a conflict they had with them. The results showed that roommates improved in three out of four of these tasks with training. They were better able to speak to their roommates about a personal problem and about a conflict they had with their roommate and were better able to listen to their roommate discuss a personal problem but not when their roommate had a conflict with them. These results suggest that communication skills training may be more effective in helping roommates to speak-up about their own concerns than listening to their roommates' concerns, but this itself is important because appropriate confrontation of one's roommate is a predictor of better college adjustment and university retention (Waldo 1986). Although this study was unique in that it focused on enhancing relationship quality among roommates, the vast majority of relationship enhancement work with college students has focused on romantic relationships.

Enhancing Relationship Quality among Romantic Relationships in College

Relationship education can be defined as the "provision of information designed to help couples and individuals experience successful, stable, romantic relationships" (Fincham, Stanley, and Rhoades 2011, 294). Relationship education is not the same as couples' therapy. Rather than treating a couple who is having significant problems in their relationship, often after their relationship has already deteriorated to a point where it may not be repairable, relationship education is aimed at preventing problems and promoting healthy relationships. Given this focus on promoting healthy relationships, relationship education is often offered to couples who are about to get married, sometimes mandated as part of religious organizations in the United States (Ooms 2005). Relationship education focuses on teaching specific skills related to communication and conflict resolution, through didactic methods, role-playing, and homework assignments.

Although it makes sense to offer relationship education to premarital couples, there is an important role for relationship education earlier in the relationship formation process, particularly aimed at emerging adult college students (Fincham, Stanley, and Rhoades 2011; Davila et al. 2016). College students are heavily involved in romantic relationships, with 57 percent of students in a relationship at any one time in college and another 29 percent desiring to be in a relationship (Fincham, Stanley, and Rhoades 2011). Moreover, college students engage in a number of unhealthy relationship behaviors, including disturbingly high levels of dating violence, hooking up behavior, where the potential for sexual victimization exists especially when alcohol is involved, and "sliding" into relationship situations, such as living together, without carefully thinking them through beforehand (Fincham, Stanley, and Rhoades 2011). Hence, college students are prime targets for relationship education programs aimed at helping them to make more clearheaded decisions and engage in constructive communication with relationship partners, thereby reducing physically and psychologically aggressive behaviors.

Project RELATE

One of the first large-scale attempts to provide relationship education to college students was called Project RELATE, conducted at the Florida State University (FSU) through a grant from the Department of Health and Human Services. The project adapted the curriculum from a widely used relationship education program, called the Prevention and Relationship Enhancement Program (PREP) (Markman, Stanley, and Blumberg 2001). PREP was modified to focus on individuals rather than couples and to target the relationship challenges of college students rather than slightly older couples, for which the program was originally developed. The curriculum was implemented as part of an introductory family relations course taught at FSU. This course is required for several majors on campus and meets liberal studies requirements, meaning that a wide cross-section of students at the university take the course. Students signed up for the course, which was then taught using two different formats. In one format, the course was a traditional lecture course, meeting three times a week, in which relationship issues were discussed as part of the course but no specific constructive communication or decision-making skills were taught as part of the course. In the second format, the students attended lecture twice a week, but then the third class period each week was turned into a breakout session where students met in small groups (of about 20 to 30 students each) with a pair of graduate student facilitators and were taught the skills of the PREP curriculum.

The PREP curriculum, targeting a number of topics of relevance to college student romantic relationships, can be seen in Table 3.2. In addition to helping students identify their relationship beliefs and explore how their personality and expectations impact their relationship behaviors, the curriculum teaches students specific communication skills, such as the speaker–listener technique and taking a "time-out" during heated arguments. Two major themes cut across the curriculum: (1) Safety in relationships—taking care of yourself and communicating safely so as to avoid physical fights; and (2) sliding versus deciding—learning how to make explicit decisions rather than just "letting things happen" in relationships, which are then regretted afterward (Fincham, Stanley, and Rhoades 2011).

Table 3.2 Curriculum of Project RELATE's relationship education program with college students

Major topics focused upon:
• Helping students become aware of their relationship beliefs and how family of origin patterns influences their view of relationships.
• Raising students' awareness of their personality characteristics and how those characteristics can both help them in a relationship and also clash with their partner.
• Helping students identify their expectations regarding relationships.
• Promoting safety in relationships by realizing expectations that cannot be appropriately addressed in an unsafe relationship.
• Learning how to break up effectively in a relationship.
Major skills taught:
• "Sliding versus Deciding"—how to make good, thoughtful decisions about relationship choices.
• Speaker–listener technique—how to communicate clearly with your partner and listen to your partner's concerns.
• Taking a "time out" when things get too heated in a discussion.
• Learning how to use XYZ communication statements.

Source: Adapted from Fincham, Stanley, and Rhoades (2011, 309–12).

Fincham and his colleagues were able to compare students who signed up for the relationship education format of this course to those in the regular lecture format on a number of variables related to better relationship functioning over the course of the semester. Students in the relationship education program were better at making decisions about their relationships and at recognizing the warning signs of a bad relationship by the end of the semester, compared with those who did not receive the relationship education portion of the course. Moreover, if these students were in a romantic relationship, they were less likely to have cheated with someone else over the course of the semester, compared with those in the regular course (Fincham, Stanley, and Rhoades 2011; Vennum and Fincham 2011).

Project RELATE demonstrated that relationship education can be successfully implemented with college students. It helped students make better relationship decisions and recognize when things might go wrong in a relationship. Also, the program allowed them to remain faithful to their romantic partners, perhaps because they were learning ways to communicate more directly with their relationship partners when they were unhappy about something in their relationship. One problem with this program is that it was quite labor-intensive, requiring a full semester-long course to complete. More recently, researchers have been exploring whether relationship education can be implemented using a computer-based platform, a modality well-suited to the lifestyle of 21st-century college students.

ePREP

The essential idea of *ePREP* is to teach the same principles of the PREP curriculum but using a self-paced slide show on the computer with video and audio components. The students watch the show, which lasts approximately 60 to 90 minutes, and complete a series of quizzes along the way to make sure they are paying attention to the material. The *ePREP* curriculum is very similar to the PREP curriculum adapted for college students, with an emphasis on dynamic factors that are associated with relationship problems, such as poor communication strategies. It teaches students specific communication and problem-solving skills, using videotaped

vignettes to demonstrate the skills, and also emphasizes enhancing positive aspects of students' relationships with their romantic partners.

The effects of *ePREP* on mental health (depression, anxiety, positive
and negative affect) and relationship outcomes (better communication
skills, relationship quality, and lowered levels of physical and psychological aggression among partners) have been evaluated in three randomized,
controlled studies with college students, two using individual students
as participants and one using pairs of romantic partners as participants
(Braithwaite and Fincham 2007, 2009, 2011). Across these studies, students who participated in the *ePREP* intervention, which included watching the slide show and then being encouraged to practice the skills learned
over a six-week period, showed significantly enhanced communication
competence and decreased verbal and physical aggressiveness toward their
romantic partner, eight weeks after the intervention had ended, and even
10 months later, when compared with participants who watched a slideshow of neutral information about relationship dynamics among college
students but did not learn any communication skills. Additionally, students in the *ePREP* condition reported less anxiety and less negative affect
over time as well, suggesting that being able to communicate more clearly
with one's romantic partner may be associated with feeling calmer and
more positive in college overall. Interestingly, Braithwaite and Fincham
(2011) found that when the *ePREP* intervention was administered to
couples simultaneously, they showed quicker and more dramatic improve-
ments in their communication competence and relationship satisfaction,
as compared to when *ePREP* was administered to only one member of the
couple relationship, where the gains in relationship quality took longer to
emerge and the couple actually did worse initially, while one member was
practicing their new communication skills on their naïve partner!

The studies reviewed previously have all focused on administering
ePREP to college students in romantic relationships (even those studies
focused on individual students required participants to be in a romantic
relationship at the time of the study). But, could learning the skills of
ePREP be useful to students not currently in a romantic relationship?
Additionally, how does administering the PREP curriculum in computerized format compare to a live version, where students learn the same
material in small groups sessions facilitated by peer facilitators? Recently,

we explored these questions in our laboratory. We randomly assigned students to receive the *ePREP* curriculum via either (1) a four-session facilitated group program, in which groups of 7 to 10 students met with two counseling graduate students and were taught the PREP curriculum using didactic instruction, role plays, and in-class exercises, or (2) the computerized *ePREP* slideshow, followed by four weeks of homework assignments in which they were required to practice the skills learned in the slide show. We also had a control group of students who watched a slideshow about relationship dynamics and rates of depression and anxiety among college students but were not taught any communication skills. Students were encouraged to participate in the study whether they were currently in a romantic relationship or not and, in fact, about 50 percent of our participants were not in a romantic relationship during the course of the study. We found that both the facilitated group condition and the computerized *ePREP* condition led to decreases in endorsement of dysfunctional relationship beliefs when compared with the control group, one and two months after the intervention was over. However, the facilitated group showed additional gains in terms of being able to make more deliberate decisions regarding relationship issues and, if they were in a romantic relationship at the time of the study, in terms of demonstrating greater mutuality with their romantic partner (Holt et al. in press). These results suggest that although *ePREP* teaches valuable skills to students, even in a computerized format, its gains may be most fully realized when the skills can be demonstrated and practiced within a live, facilitated format, although that format need not be as intensive or last the full length of a semester, as in *Project RELATE*.

Summary and Conclusions

Chapter 3 has reviewed the important role that primary prevention interventions can play in helping students make a smooth transition to college and to enhance their social and emotional well-being throughout their college experience, especially by learning more effective communication skills with their roommates and romantic partners. These interventions are relatively low-cost, can be administered to groups of students at a time, often as part of a class or extended orientation program (or on the computer), and are facilitated by para-professional peer educators, who share many of the same experiences of the students involved in the programs. These programs hold great promise for reaching a wide cross-section of students who would not traditionally seek counseling services but who may struggle with the challenges of adjusting to college and negotiating tricky roommate and romantic relationship situations. Given their appeal, a number of universities, like Queens University in Charlotte, have adopted some kind of primary prevention intervention program to aid students in transitioning to college, beyond just the traditional initial orientation programs offered by almost all universities. These primary prevention intervention programs will be especially important in addressing the mental health needs of college students in the years to come, given the increasing symptomatic distress of students attending college today and the limited resources of most college counseling centers. University administrators and higher education personnel would be wise to support research on the development and efficacy of such programs.

References

Abaied, J., and C. Emond. 2013. "Parent Psychological Control and Responses to Interpersonal Stress in Emerging Adulthood: Moderating Effects of Behavioral Inhibition and Behavioral Activation." *Emerging Adulthood* 1, no. 4, pp. 258–70.

Ainsworth, M., M. Blehar, E. Waters, and S. Wall. 1978/2015. *Patterns of Attachment: A Psychological Study of the Strange Situation.* New York: Routledge.

Allport, G. 1954. *The Nature of Prejudice.* Reading, MA: Addison-Wesley.

Ames, M., M. Pratt, S. Pancer, M. Wintre, J. Polivy, S. Birnie-Lefcovitch, and G. Adams. 2011. "The Moderating Effects of Attachment Style on Students' Experience of a Transition to University Group Facilitation Program." *Canadian Journal of Behavioural Sciences* 43, no. 1, pp. 1–12.

Armsden, G., and M. Greenberg. 1987. "The Inventory of Parent and Peer Attachment: Individual Differences and Their Relationship to Psychological Well-being in Adolescence." *Journal of Youth and Adolescence* 16, no. 5, pp. 427–54.

Arshad, A., and F. Naz. 2014. "Inter-Parental Conflict, Parental Rejection, and Personality Maladjustment in University Students." *Journal of Behavioral Sciences* 24, no. 2, pp. 83–99.

Bahns, A., C. Crandall, A. Canevello, and J. Crocker. 2013. "Deciding to Dissolve: Individual and Relationship-Level Predictors of Roommate Breakup." *Basic and Applied Social Psychology* 35, no. 2, pp. 164–75.

Banker, J., C. Kaestle, and K. Allen. 2010. "Dating Is Hard Work: A Narrative Approach To Understanding Sexual and Romantic Relationships in Young Adulthood." *Contemporary Family Therapy* 32, no. 2, pp. 173–91.

Barber, B. 1996. "Parental Psychological Control: Revisiting a Neglected Construct." *Child Development* 67, no. 6, pp. 3296–319.

Baumrind, D. 1971. "Current Patterns of Parental Authority." *Developmental Psychology Monographs* 4, no. 1(p2), pp. 99–102.

Baumrind, D. 1989. "Rearing Competent Children." In *New direction for Child Development: Child Development, Today and Tomorrow*, ed. W. Damon, 349–78. San Francisco: Jossey-Bass.

Bell, K., J. Allen, S. Hauser, and T. O'Conner. 1996. "Family Factors and Young Adult Transitions: Educational Attainment and Occupational Prestige." In *Transitions Through adolescence: Interpersonal Domains and Context*, eds. J. Graber, J. Brooks-Gunn, and A. Peterson, 345–66. Hillsdale, NJ: Erlbaum.

Berg, J. 1984. "Development of Friendship Between Roommates." *Journal of Personality and Social Psychology* 46, no. 2, pp. 346–56.

Bjorklund, S., J. Parente, and D. Sathianathan. 2004. "Effects of Faculty Interaction and Feedback on Gains in Student Skills." *Journal of Engineering Education* 93, no. 2, pp. 153–60.

Blazina, C., and C. Watkins. 1996. "Masculine Gender Role Conflict: Effects on College Men's Psychological Well-Being, Chemical Substance Usage, and Attitudes Toward Help-Seeking." *Journal of Counseling Psychology* 43, no. 4, pp. 461–65.

Blazina, C., and C. Watkins. 2000. "Separation/Individuation, Parental Attachment, and Male Gender Role Conflict: Attitudes Toward the Feminine and the Fragile Masculine Self." *Psychology of Men and Masculinity* 1, no. 2, pp. 126–32.

Blustein, D., M. Walbridge, M. Friedlander, and D. Palladino. 1991. "Contributions of Psychological Separation and Parental Attachment to the Career Development Process." *Journal of Counseling Psychology* 38, no. 1, pp. 39–50.

Bowlby, J. 1969/1982. *Attachment and Loss: Vol. 1. Attachment.* New York: Basic Books.

Brack, G., M. Gay, and K. Matheny. 1993. "Relationships Between Attachment and Coping Resources Among Late Adolescents." *Journal of College Student Development* 34, no. 3, pp. 212–15.

Braithwaite, S., and F. Fincham. 2007. "ePREP: Computer Based Prevention of Relationship Dysfunction, Depression and Anxiety." *Journal of Social and Clinical Psychology* 26, no. 5, pp. 609–22.

Braithwaite, S., and F. Fincham. 2009. "A Randomized Clinical Trial of a Computer Based Preventive Intervention: Replication and Extension of ePREP." *Journal of Family Psychology* 23, no. 1, pp. 32–38.

Braithwaite, S., and F. Fincham. 2011. "Computer-Based Dissemination: A Randomized Clinical Trial of ePREP Using the Actor Partner Interdependence Model." *Behaviour Research and Therapy* 49, no. 2, pp. 126–31.

Braithwaite, S., R. Delevi, and F. Fincham. 2010. "Romantic Relationships and the Physical and Mental Health of College Students." *Personal Relationships* 17, no. 1, pp. 1–12.

Buhrmester, D., W. Furman, M. Wittenberg, and H. Reis. 1988. "Five Domains of Interpersonal Competence in Peer Relationships." *Journal of Personality and Social Psychology* 55, no. 6, pp. 991–1008.

Carranza, L., P. Kilmann, and J. Vendemia. 2009. "Links Between Parent Characteristics and Attachment Variables for College Students of Parental Divorce." *Adolescence* 44, no. 174, pp. 253–71.

Chickering, A., and L. Reisser. 1993. *Education and Identity.* 2nd ed. San Francisco, CA: Jossey-Bass.

Conley, C., J. Durlak, and A. Kirsch. 2015. "A Meta-Analysis of Universal Mental Health Prevention Programs for Higher Education Students." *Prevention Science* 16, no. 4, pp. 487–507.

Conley, C., L. Travers, and F. Bryant. 2013. "Promoting Psychosocial Adjustment and Stress Management in First-Year College Students: The Benefits of Engagement in a Psychosocial Wellness Seminar." *Journal of American College Health* 61, no. 2, pp. 75–86.

Cox, B., K. McIntosh, P. Terenzini, R. Reason, B. Quaye. 2010. "Pedagogical Signals of Faculty Approachability: Factors Shaping Faculty-Student Interaction Outside the Classroom." *Research in Higher Education* 51, no. 8, pp. 767–88.

Coyne, J., M. Rohrbaugh, V. Shoham, J. Sonnega, J. Nicklas, and J. Cranford. 2001. "Prognostic Importance of Marital Quality for Survival of Congestive Heart Failure." *American Journal of Cardiology* 88, no. 5, pp. 526–29.

Cui, M., and F. Fincham. 2010. "The Differential Effects of Parental Divorce and Marital Conflict on Young Adult Romantic Relationships." *Personal Relationships* 17, no. 3, pp. 331–43.

Davila, J., V. Bhatia, J. Latack, L. Mize, and J. Zhou. 2016. *Healthy Relationships Workshop for Emerging Adults: Development and Preliminary Data.* Paper Presented at the Bi-Annual Meeting of the Society for Research on Adolescence, Baltimore, MD.

Davila, J., J. Mattanah, V. Bhatia, J. Latack, B. Feinstein, N. Eaton, J. Daks, S. Kumar, E. Lomash, M. McCormick, and J. Zhou. (in press). "Romantic Competence, Healthy Relationship Functioning, and Well-Being in Emerging Adults." *Personal Relationships.*

Davila, J., S. Steinberg, L. Kachadourian, R. Cobb, and F. Fincham. 2004. "Romantic Involvement and Depressive Symptoms in Early and Late Adolescence: The Role of Preoccupied Relational Style." *Personal Relationships* 11, no. 2, pp. 161–78.

Davila, J., S. Steinberg, M. Miller, C. Stroud, L. Starr, and A. Yoneda. 2009. "Assessing Romantic Competence in Adolescence: The Romantic Competence Interview." *Journal of Adolescence* 32, no. 1, pp. 55–75.

DeBard, R., and C. Sacks. 2011–2012. "Greek Membership: The Relationship with First-Year Academic Performance." *Journal of College Student Retention* 13, no. 1, pp. 109–26.

DeFranc W., and J. Mahalik. 2002. "Masculine Gender Role Conflict and Stress in Relation to Parental Attachment and Separation." *Psychology of Men and Masculinity* 3, no. 1, pp. 51–60.

Degges-White, S., and C. Borzumato-Gainey. 2014. *College Student Mental Health Counseling: A Developmental Approach.* New York: Springer Publishing.

Duncan, G., J. Boisjoly, M. Kremer, D. Levy, and J. Eccles. 2005. "Peer Effects in Drug Use and Sex Among College Students." *Journal of Abnormal Child Psychology* 33, no. 3, pp. 375–85.

Dusselier, L., B. Dunn, Y. Wang, M. Shelley, and D. Whalen. 2005. "Personal, Health, Academic, and Environmental Predictors of Stress for Residence Hall Students." *Journal of American College Health* 54, no. 1, pp. 15–24.

Eisenberg, M., D. Ackard, M. Resnick, and D. Neumark-Sztainer. 2009. "Casual Sex and Psychological Health Among Young Adults: Is Having 'Friends with Benefits' Emotional Damaging?" *Perspectives on Sexual and Reproductive Health* 41, no. 4, pp. 231–37.

Erdur-Baker, O., C. Aberson, J. Barrow, and M. Draper. 2006. "Nature and Severity of College Students' Psychological Concerns: A Comparison of Clinical and Nonclinical National Samples." *Professional Psychology: Research and Practice* 37, no. 3, pp. 317–23.

Erikson, E. 1968. *Identity: Youth and Crisis.* New York: Norton.

Faber, A., A. Edwards, K. Bauer, and J. Wetchler. 2003. "Family Structure. Its Effects on Adolescent Attachment and Identity Formation." *The American Journal of Family Therapy* 31, no. 4, pp. 243–55.

Fass M., and J. Tubman. 2002. "The Influence of Parental and Peer Attachment on College Students' Academic Achievement." *Psychology in the Schools* 39, no. 5, pp. 561–74.

Feagin, J., V. Hera, and N. Imani. 1996. *The Agony of Education: Black Students at White Colleges and Universities.* New York: Nikitah Publications.

Feenstra, J., V. Banyard, E. Rines, and K. Hopkins. 2001. "First Year Students' Adaptation to College: The Role of Family Variables and Individual Coping." *Journal of College Student Development* 42, no. 2, pp. 106–13.

Felsman, D., and D. Blustein. 1999. "The Role of Peer Relatedness in Late Adolescent Career Development." *Journal of Vocational Behavior* 54, no. 2, pp. 279–95.

Fielder, R., K. Carey, and M. Carey. 2013. "Are Hookups Replacing Romantic Relationships? A Longitudinal Study of First-Year Female College Students." *Journal of Adolescent Health* 52, no. 2, pp. 657–59.

Fincham, F., S. Stanley, and G. Rhoades. 2011. "Relationship Education in Emerging Adulthood: Problems and Prospects." In *Romantic Relationships in Emerging Adulthood,* eds. F. Fincham, and M. Cui, 293–333. Cambridge, UK: Cambridge University Press.

Fleming, C., H. White, S. Oesterle, K. Haggerty, and R. Catalano. 2010. "Romantic Relationship Status Changes and Substance Use Among 18 to 20-year-Olds." *Journal of Studies on Alcohol and Drugs* 71, no. 6, pp. 847–56.

Foderaro, L. 2010. "Roommates Who Click." *The New York Times*, August 20. www.nytimes.com/2010/08/22/nyregion/22roommates.html?_r=0

Gabriel, T. 2010. "Students, Welcome to College; Parents, Go Home." *The New York Times, August 22.*

Gaither, S., and S. Sommers. 2013. "Living with an Other-Race Roommate Shapes Whites' Behavior in Subsequent Diverse Settings." *Journal of Experimental Social Psychology* 49, no. 2, pp. 272–76.

Gerst, M., and H. Sweetwood. 1973. "Correlates of Dormitory Social Climate." *Environment and Behavior* 5, no. 4, pp. 440–64.

Glindemann, K., and E. Geller. 2003. "A Systematic Assessment of Intoxication at University Parties: Effects of the Environmental Context." *Environment and Behavior* 35, no. 5, pp. 655–64.

Gore, J., S. Cross, and M. Morris. 2006. "Let's Be Friends: Relational Self-Construal and the Development of Intimacy." *Personal Relationships* 13, no. 1, pp. 83–102.

Graham, S., J. Huang, M. Clark, and V. Helgeson. 2008. "The Positives of Negative Emotions: Willingness to Express Negative Emotions Promotes Relationships." *Personality and Social Psychology Bulletin* 34, no. 3, pp. 394–406.

Grantham, A., E. Robinson, and D. Chapman. 2015. "That Truly Meant a Lot to Me": A Qualitative Examination of Meaningful Faculty-Student Interactions. *College Teaching* 63, no. 3, pp. 125–32.

Green, J., and A. King. 2009. "Domestic Violence and Parental Divorce as Predictors of Best Friendship Qualities Among College Students." *Journal of Divorce and Remarriage* 50, no. 2, pp. 100–18.

Greenberger, E., and C. McLaughlin. 1998. "Attachment, Coping, and Explanatory Style in Late Adolescence." *Journal of Youth and Adolescence* 27, no. 2, pp. 121–39.

Grych, J., M. Seid, and F. Fincham. 1992. "Assessing Marital Conflict from the Child's Perspective: The Children's Perception of Interparental Conflict Scale." *Child Development* 63, no. 3, pp. 558–72.

Guiffrida, D. 2005. "Othermothering as a Framework for Understanding African American Students' Definitions of Student-Centered Faculty." *The Journal of Higher Education* 76, no. 6, pp. 702–23.

Hanasono, L., and L. Nadler. 2012. "A Dialectical Approach to Rethinking Roommate Relationships." *Journal of College Student Development* 53, no. 5, pp. 623–35.

Hannum, J., and D. Dvorak. 2004. "Effects of Family Conflict, Divorce, and Attachment Patterns on the Psychological Distress and Social Adjustment of College Freshmen." *Journal of College Student Development* 45, no. 1, pp. 27–42.

Harper, M., and C. Allegretti. 2009. "Transition to University: An Adjustment and Retention Program for First-Year Students." *National Resource Center for the First-Year Experience and Students in Transition* 6, pp. 10–12.

Harper, M., and C. Allegretti. 2013. "Expanding a Peer-Facilitation Program Beyond the Fall Term." *National Resource Center for the First-Year Experience and Students in Transition* 11, pp. 16–17.

Harter, S. 1988. *Self-Perception Profile for Adolescent: Manual and Questionnaires.* Colorado: University of Denver.

Hays, R., and D. Oxley. 1986. "Social Network Development and Functioning During a Life Transition." *Journal of Personality and Social Psychology* 50, no. 2, pp. 305–13.

Hevel, M., G. Martin, D. Weeden, and E. Pascarella. 2015. "The Effects of Fraternity and Sorority Membership in the Fourth Year of College: A Detrimental or Value-Added Component of Undergraduate Education?" *Journal of College Student Development* 56, no. 5, pp. 456–70.

Holt, L. 2014. "Help Seeking and Social Competence Mediate the Parental Attachment-College Adjustment Relation." *Personal Relationships* 21, no. 4, pp. 640–54.

Holt, L., J. Mattanah, C. Schmidt, J. Daks, E. Brophy, P. Minnaar, and K. Rorer. (in press). "Effects of Relationship Education on Emerging Adults' Relationship Beliefs and Behaviors." *Personal Relationships.*

Jacobson, K., and L. Crockett. 2000. "Parental Monitoring and Adolescent Adjustment: An Ecological Perspective." *Journal of Research on Adolescence* 10, no. 1, pp. 65–97.

Jamison, T., and L. Ganong. 2011. "'We're Not Living Together': Stayover Relationships Among College-Educated Emerging Adults." *Journal of Social and Personal Relationships* 28, no. 4, pp. 536–57.

Jamison, T., and C. Proulx. 2013. "Stayovers in Emerging Adulthood: Who Stays Over and Why?" *Personal Relationships* 20, no. 1, pp. 155–69.

Joyce, A. 2014. "How Helicopter Parents are Ruining College Students." *The Washington Post,* September 2. www.washingtonpost.com/news/parenting/wp/2014/09/02/how-helicopter-parents-are-ruining-college-students

Joyce, A. 2015. "What Exactly Is This Whole 'Free-Range Kid' Thing?" *The Washington Post,* May 26. www.washingtonpost.com/news/parenting/wp/2015/05/26/what-exactly-is-this-whole-free-range-kid-thing

Kenny, M. 1987. "The Extent and Function of Parental Attachment Among First-Year College Students." *Journal of Youth and Adolescence* 16, no. 1, pp. 17–28.

Kenny, M., and G. Donaldson. 1991. "Contributions of Parental Attachment and Family Structure to the Social and Psychological Functioning of First-Year College Students." *Journal of Counseling Psychology* 38, no. 4, pp. 479–86.

Kenny, M., and K. Rice. 1995. "Attachment to Parents and Adjustment in Late Adolescent College Students: Current Status, Applications, and Future Considerations." *The Counseling Psychologist* 23, no. 3, pp. 433–56.

Kenny, M. 1990. "College Seniors' Perceptions of Parental Attachments: The Value and Stability of Family Ties." *Journal of College Student Development* 31, 39–45.

Kilgannon, S., and T. Erwin. 1992. "A Longitudinal Study about the Identity and Moral Development of Greek Students." *Journal of College Student Development* 33, no. 3, pp. 253–59.

Kim, Y., and L. Sax. 2009. "Student-Faculty Interaction in Research Universities: Differences by Student Gender, Race, Social Class, and First-Generation Status." *Research in Higher Education* 50, no. 5, pp. 206–18.

Kim, Y., and L. Sax. 2014. "The Effects of Student-Faculty Interaction on Academic Self-Concept: Does Academic Major Matter?" *Research in Higher Education* 55, no. 8, pp. 780–809.

Kuh, G., and S. Hu. 2001. "The Effects of Student-Faculty Interactions in the 1990s." *The Review of Higher Education* 24, no. 3, pp. 309–32.

Kumar, S., and J. Mattanah (in press). "Parental Attachment, Romantic Competence, Relationship Satisfaction, and Psychosocial Adjustment in Emerging Adulthood." *Personal Relationships.*

Lamborn, S., N. Mounts, L. Steinberg, and S. Dornbusch. 1991. "Patterns of Competence and Adjustment Among Adolescents from Authoritative, Authoritarian, Indulgent, and Neglectful Families." *Child Development* 62, no. 5, pp. 1049–65.

Larose S., and A. Bernier. 2001. "Social Support Processes: Mediators of Attachment State of Mind and Adjustment in Late Adolescence." *Attachment and Human Development* 3, no. 1, pp. 96–120.

Larose, S., M. Boivin, and A. Doyle. 2001. "Parental Representations and Attachment Style as Predictors of Support-Seeking Behaviors and Perceptions of Support in an Academic Counseling Relationship." *Personal Relationships* 8, no. 1, pp. 93–113.

Lepore, S. 1992. "Social Conflict, Social Support, and Psychological Distress: Evidence of Cross-Domain Buffering Effects." *Journal of Personality and Social Psychology* 63, no. 5, pp. 857–67.

Lillard, L., and L. Waite. 1995. "Till Death Do Us Part: Marital Disruption and Mortality." *American Journal of Sociology* 100, no. 5, pp. 1131–56.

Lillis, M. 2011–2012. "Faculty Emotional Intelligence and Student-Faculty Interactions: Implications for Student Retention." *Journal of College Student Retention* 13, no. 2, pp. 155–78.

Lopez, F. 1997. "Student–Professor Relationship Styles, Childhood Attachment Bonds and Current Academic Orientations." *Journal of Social and Personal Relationships* 14, no. 2, pp. 271–82.

Lopez, F., V. Campbell, and C. Watkins. 1988. "Family Structure, Psychological Separation, and College Adjustment: A Canonical Analysis and Cross-Validation." *Journal of Counseling Psychology* 35, no. 4, pp. 402–9.

Lopez, F., V. Campbell, and C. Watkins. 1989. "Effects of Marital Conflict and Family Coalition Patterns on College Student Adjustment." *Journal of College Student Development* 30, pp. 46–52.

Love, K., and T. Murdock. 2004. "Attachment to Parents and Psychological Well-Being: An Examination of Young Adult College Students in Intact Families and Stepfamilies." *Journal of Family Psychology* 18, no. 4, pp. 600–8.

Lucas-Thompson, R. and C. Hostinar. 2013. "Family Income and Appraisals of Parental Conflict as Predictors of Psychological Adjustment and Diurnal Cortisol in Emerging Adulthood." *Journal of Family Psychology* 27, no. 5, pp. 784–94.

Marano, H. 2010. "Have College Freshmen Changed." *The New York Times*, October.

Marano, H. 2014. "Helicopter Parenting—It's Worse Than You Think." *Psychology Today*, January 31. www.psychologytoday.com/blog/nation-wimps/201401/helicopter-parenting-its-worse-you-think

Markiewicz, D., H. Lawford, A. Doyle, and N. Haggart. 2006. "Developmental Differences in Adolescents' and Young Adults' Use of Mothers, Fathers, Best Friends, and Romantic Partners to Fulfill Attachment Needs." *Journal of Youth and Adolescence* 35, no. 1, pp. 127–40.

Markman, H., S. Stanley, and S. Blumberg. 2001. *Fighting for Your Marriage*. San Francisco: Jossey-Bass.

Mattanah, J.F. 2016. *College Student Psychological Adjustment: Theory, Methods, and Statistical Trends*. New York: Momentum Press.

Mattanah, J., J. Ayers, B. Brand, L. Brooks, J. Quimby, and S. McNary. 2010. "A Social Support Intervention to Ease the College Transition: Exploring Main Effects and Moderators." *Journal of College Student Development* 51, no. 1, pp. 93–108.

Mattanah, J., L. Brooks, B. Brand, J. Quimby, and J. Ayers. 2012. "A Social Support Intervention and Academic Achievement in College: Does Perceived Loneliness Mediate the Relationship?" *Journal of College Counseling* 15, no. 1, pp. 22–36.

Minuchin, S. 1974. *Families and Family Therapy*. Cambridge, MA: Harvard University Press.

National Council of Educational Statistics. 2014. *The Condition of Education*. U.S. Department of Education, Washington, DC. Retrieved from www.nces.ed.gov.

Nelson, L., L. Padilla-Walker, and M. Nielson. 2015. "Is Hovering Smothering or Loving? An Examination of Parental Warmth as a Moderator of Relations Between Helicopter Parenting and Emerging Adults' Indices of Adjustment." *Emerging Adulthood*, no. 3, pp. 282–85.

Nelson, L., L. Padilla-Walker, K. Christensen, C. Evans, and J. Carroll. 2011. "Parenting in Emerging Adulthood: An Examination of Parenting Clusters and Correlates." *Journal of Youth and Adolescence* 40, no. 6, pp. 730–43.

Nettles, M. 1991. "Racial Similarities and Differences in the Predictors of College Student Achievement." In *College in Black and White*, eds. W. Allen, E. Epps, and N. Haniff, 75–94. Albany, NY: State University of NY Press.

Ooms, T. 2005. *The New Kid on the Block: What Is Marriage Education and Does It Work?* Washington, DC: Center for Law and Social Policy.

Oswald, D., and E. Clark. 2003. "Best Friends Forever? High School Best Friendships and the Transition to College." *Personal Relationships* 10, no. 2, pp. 187–96.

Owen, J., and F. Fincham. 2011. "Young adults' Emotional Reactions After Hooking Up Encounters." *Archives of Sexual Behavior* 40, no. 2, pp. 321–30.

Owen, J., F. Fincham, and J. Moore. 2011. "Short-Term Prospective Study of Hooking up Among College Students." *Archives of Sexual Behavior* 40, no. 2, pp. 331–41.

Owen, J., G. Rhoades, S. Stanley, and F. Fincham. 2010. "Hooking up Among College Students: Demographic and Psychosocial Correlates." *Archives of Sexual Behavior* 39, no. 3, pp. 653–63.

Pace, T. 1970. "Roommate Dissatisfaction in Residence Halls." *Journal of College Student Personnel* 11, no. 2, pp. 144–47.

Padilla-Walker, L., and L. Nelson. 2012. "Black Hawk Down: Establishing Helicopter Parenting As a Distinct Construct from Other Forms of Parental Control During Emerging Adulthood." *Journal of Adolescence* 35, no. 5, pp. 1177–90.

Padilla-Walker, L., L. Nelson, S. Madsen, and C. Barry. 2008. "The Role of Perceived Knowledge on Emerging Adults' Risk Behaviors." *Journal of Youth and Adolescence* 37, no. 7, pp. 847–59.

Parade, S., E. Leerkes, and A. Blankson. 2010. "Attachment to Parents, Social Anxiety, and Close relationships of Female Students Over the Transition to College." *Journal of Youth and Adolescence* 39, no. 2, pp. 127–37.

Park, J. 2014. "Clubs and the Campus racial Climate: Student Organizations and Interracial Friendship in College." *Journal of College Student Development* 55, no. 7, pp. 641–60.

Pascarella, E., and P. Terenzini. 1977. "Patterns of Student-Faculty Informal Interaction Beyond the Classroom and Voluntary Freshmen Attrition." *The Journal of Higher Education* 48, pp. 540–52.

Pascarella, E., and P. Terenzini. 1978. "Student-Faculty Informal Relationships and Classroom and Freshmen Year Educational Outcomes." *The Journal of Educational Research* 71, no. 4, pp. 183–89.

Pascarella, E., and P. Terenzini. 1980. "Student-Faculty and Student-Peer Relationships as Mediators of the Structural Effects of Undergraduate Residence Arrangements." *The Journal of Educational Research* 73, no. 6, pp. 344–53.

Pascarella, E., and P. Terenzini. 2005. *How College Affects Students: A Third Decade of Research.* vol. 2. San Francisco, CA: Jossey-Bass.

Pascarella, E., M. Edison, E. Whitt, A. Nora, L. Hagedon, and P. Terenzini. 1996. "Cognitive Effects of Greek Affiliation During the First Year of College." *NASPA Journal* 33, no. 4, pp. 242–59.

Paul, E., and S. Brier. 2001. "Friendsickness in the transition to College: Precollege Predictors and College Adjustment Correlates." *Journal of Counseling and Development* 79, no. 1, pp. 77–89.

Paul, E., and M. Kelleher. 1995. "Precollege Concerns About Losing and Making Friends in College: Implications for Friendship Satisfaction and Self-Esteem During the College Transition." *Journal of College Student Development* 36, pp. 513–20.

Pettigrew, T. 1998. "Intergroup Contact Theory." *Annual Review of Psychology* 49, no. 1, pp. 65–85.

Pittman, L., and A. Richmond. 2008. "University Belonging, Friendship Quality, and Psychological Adjustment During the Transition to College." *The Journal of Experimental Education* 76, no. 4, pp. 343–61.

Pratt, M., B. Hunsberger, S. Pancer, S. Alisat, C. Bowers, K. Mackey, A. Ostaniewicz, E. Rog, B. Terzian, and N. Thomas. 2000. "Facilitating the Transition to University: Evaluation of a Social Support Discussion Intervention Program." *Journal of College Student Development* 41, pp. 427–41.

Puentes, J., D. Knox, and M. Zusman. 2008. "Participants in 'Friends with Benefits' Relationships." *College Student Journal* 42, no. 1, pp. 176–80.

Ranney, J., and W. Troop-Gordon. 2012. "Computer-Mediated Communication with Distant Friends: Relations with Adjustment During Students' First Semester in College." *Journal of Educational Psychology* 104, no. 3, pp. 848–61.

Reis, H., and P. Shaver. 1988. "Intimacy as an Interpersonal Process. "In *Handbook of Personal Relationships,* ed. S. Duck, 367–89. Chichester, UK: Wiley.

Rhoades, G., and L. Wood. 2014. "Family Conflict and College-Student Social Adjustment: The Mediating Role of Emotional Distress About the Family." *Couple and Family Psychology: Research and Practice* 3, no. 3, pp. 156–64.

Rice K., and T. Whaley. 1993. "A Short-Term Longitudinal Study of Within-Semester Stability and Change in Attachment and College Student Adjustment." *Journal of College Student Development* 35, pp. 324–30.

Sacerdote, B. 2001. "Peer Effects with Random Assignment: Results for Dartmouth Roommates." *The Quarterly Journal of Economics* 116, pp. 681–703.

Saferstein, J., G. Neimeyer, and C. Hagans. 2005. "Attachment as a Predictor of Friendship Qualities in College Youth." *Social Behavior and Personality* 33, no. 8, pp. 767–76.

Salvatore, J., K. Kendler, and D. Dick. 2014. "Romantic Relationship Status and Alcohol Use and Problems Across the First Year of College." *Journal of Studies on Alcohol and Drugs* 75, no. 4, pp. 580–89.

Schiffrin, H., M. Liss, H. McLean, K. Geary, M. Erchull, and T. Tashner. 2014. "Helping or Hovering: The Effects of Helicopter Parenting on College Students' Well-Being." *Journal of Child and Family Studies* 23, no. 3, pp. 548–57.

Scott, A., and B. Mallinckrodt. 2005. "Parental Emotional Support, Science Self-Efficacy, and Choice of Science Major in Undergraduate Women." *The Career Development Quarterly* 53, no. 3, pp. 263–73.

Segrin, C., and L. Abramson. 1994. "Negative Reactions to Depressive Behaviors: A Communication Theories Analysis." *Journal of Abnormal Psychology* 103, no. 4, pp. 655–68.

Shook, N., and R. Fazio. 2008a. "Roommate Relationships: A Comparison of Interracial and Same-Race Living Situations." *Group Processes and Intergroup Relations* 11, no. 4, pp. 425–37.

Shook, N., and R. Fazio. 2008b. "Interracial Roommate Relationships: An Experimental Test of the Contact Hypothesis." *Psychological Science* 19, no. 7, pp. 717–23.

Shulman, S., and J. Connolly. 2013. "The Challenge of Romantic Relationships in Emerging Adulthood: Reconceptualization of the Field." *Emerging Adulthood* 1, no. 1, pp. 27–39.

Siebenbruner, J. 2013. "Are College Students Replacing Dating and Romantic Relationships with Hooking up?" *Journal of College Student Development* 54, no. 4, pp. 433–38.

Sorokou, C., and C. Weissbrod. 2005. "Men and Women's Attachment and Contact Patterns with Parents During the First Year of College." *Journal of Youth and Adolescence* 34, no. 3, pp. 221–28.

Steinberg, L., J. Elmen, and N. Mounts. 1989. "Authoritative Parenting, Psychosocial Maturity, and Academic Success Among Adolescents." *Child Development* 60, pp. 1424–36.

Stinebrickner, R., and T. Stinebrickner. 2006. "What Can Be Learned About Peer Effects Using College Roommates? Evidence from New Survey Data and Students from Disadvantaged Backgrounds." *Journal of Public Economics* 90, no. 8, pp. 1435–54.

Strage, A., and T. Brandt. 1999. "Authoritative Parenting and College Students' Academic Adjustment and Success." *Journal of Educational Psychology* 91, no. 1, pp. 146–56.

Strokoff, J., J. Owen, and F. Fincham. 2015. "Diverse Reactions to Hooking Up Among U.S. University Students." *Archives of Sexual Behavior* 44, no. 4, pp. 935–43.

Thériault, A. 2015. "The Problem with Fraternity Rape Culture Is Even Bigger than You Think." *The Daily Dot*, October 22. www.dailydot.com/opinion/fraternity-rush-week-selfie-boobs-toxic/

Tinto, V. 1993. *Leaving College: Rethinking the Causes and Cures of Student Attrition*. 2nd ed. Chicago: University of Chicago Press.

Trinke, S., and K. Bartholomew. 1997. "Hierarchies of Attachment Relationships in Young Adulthood." *Journal of Social and Personal Relationships* 14, no. 5, pp. 603–25.

Urry, S., L. Nelson, and L. Padilla-Walker. 2011. "Mother Knows Best: Psychological Control, Child Disclosure, and Maternal Knowledge in Emerging Adulthood." *Journal of Family Studies* 17, no. 2, pp. 157–73.

Van Laar, C., S. Levin, S. Sinclair, and J. Sidanius. 2005. "The Effect of University Roommate Contact on Ethnic Attitudes and Behavior." *Journal of Experimental Social Psychology* 41, no. 4, pp. 329–45.

VanderDrift, L., J. Lehmiller, and J. Kelly. 2012. "Commitment in Friends with Benefits Relationships: Implications for Relational and Safe-Sex Outcomes." *Personal Relationships* 19, no. 1, pp. 1–13.

Vennum, A., and F. Fincham. 2011. "Assessing Decision Making in Young Adult Romantic Relationships." *Psychological Assessment* 23, no. 3, pp. 739–51.

Waldo, M. 1984. "Roommate Communication as Related to Students' Personal and Social Adjustment." *Journal of College Student Personnel* 25, no. 1, pp. 39–44.

Waldo, M. 1985. "Improving Interpersonal Communication in a University Residential Community." *Journal of Humanistic Education and Development* 23, no. 3, pp. 126–33.

Waldo, M. 1986. "Academic achievement and Retention as Related to Students' Personal and Social Adjustment." *Journal of College and University Student Housing* 16, no. 1, pp. 19–23.

Waldo, M. 1989. "Primary Prevention in University Residence Halls: Paraprofessional-led Relationship Enhancement Groups for College Roommates." *Journal of Counseling and Development* 67, pp. 465–71.

Waldo, M., and A. Furman. 1981. "Roommate Relationships, Communication Skills, and Psychological Adjustment in Residence Halls." *The Journal of College and University Student Housing* 11, no. 1, pp. 31–35.

Wechsler, H., J. Lee, G. Kuh, and H. Lee. 2000. "College Binge Drinking in the 1990s: A Continuing Problem." *Journal of American College Health* 48, no. 5, pp. 199–210.

Weiss, L., and J. Schwarz. 1996. "The Relationship Between Parenting Types and Older Adolescents' Personality, Academic Achievement, Adjustment, and Substance Use." *Child Development* 67, no. 5, pp. 2101–14.

Welsh, D., C. Grello, and M. Harper. 2003. "When Love Hurts: Depression and Adolescent Romantic Relationships." In *Adolescent Romantic relations and Sexual Behavior: Theory, Research, and Practical Implications,* ed. P. Florsheim, 185–212. Mahwah, NJ: Lawrence Erlbaum.

Whisman, M., and R. Kaiser. 2008. "Marriage and Relationship Issues." In *Risk Factors in Depression,* eds. K. Dobson, and D. Dozois, 363–84. Oxford, England: Elsevier.

Whitton, S., and A. Kuryluk. 2012. "Relationship Satisfaction and Depressive Symptoms in Emerging Adults: Cross-Sectional Associations and Moderating Effects of Relationship Characteristics." *Journal of Family Psychology* 26, no. 2, pp. 226–35.

Whitton, S., E. Weitbrecht, A. Kuryluk, and M. Bruner. 2013. "Committed Dating Relationships and Mental Health Among College Students." *Journal of American College Health* 61, no. 3, pp. 176–83.

Willoughby, B., J. Hersh, L. Padilla-Walker, and L. Nelson. 2015. "Back Off! Helicopter Parenting and a Retreat from Marriage Among Emerging Adults." *Journal of Family Issues* 36, pp. 669–92.

Wilson, R., L. Woods, and J. Gaff. 1974. "Social-Psychological Accessibility and Faculty-Student Interaction Beyond the Classroom." *Sociology of Education* 47, no. 1, pp. 74–92.

Wintre, M., and M. Yaffe. 2000. "First-Year Students' Adjustment to University Life as a Function of Relationships with Parents." *Journal of Adolescent Research* 15, no. 1, pp. 9–37.

Index

TITLES FROM OUR PSYCHOLOGY COLLECTION

Children's Rights: Towards Social Justice
by Anne B. Smith

The Elements of Mental Tests, Second Edition
by John D. Mayer

Momentum Press is one of the leading book publishers in the field of engineering, mathematics, health, and applied sciences. Momentum Press offers over 30 collections, including Aerospace, Biomedical, Civil, Environmental, Nanomaterials, Geotechnical, and many others.

Momentum Press is actively seeking collection editors as well as authors. For more information about becoming an MP author or collection editor, please visit http://www.momentumpress.net/contact

Announcing Digital Content Crafted by Librarians

Momentum Press offers digital content as authoritative treatments of advanced engineering topics by leaders in their field. Hosted on ebrary, MP provides practitioners, researchers, faculty, and students in engineering, science, and industry with innovative electronic content in sensors and controls engineering, advanced energy engineering, manufacturing, and materials science.

Momentum Press offers library-friendly terms:

- perpetual access for a one-time fee
- no subscriptions or access fees required
- unlimited concurrent usage permitted
- downloadable PDFs provided
- free MARC records included
- free trials

The **Momentum Press** digital library is very affordable, with no obligation to buy in future years.

For more information, please visit **www.momentumpress.net/library** or to set up a trial in the US, please contact **mpsales@globalepress.com**.

www.ingramcontent.com/pod-product-compliance
Lightning Source LLC
Chambersburg PA
CBHW050538270326

41926CB00015B/3281